C000068123

AN ILLUSTRATED HISTORY

OF THE

SOCIETY OF DORSET MEN

compiled by Rev. Dr. JohnTravell, FRSA

First published in Great Britain in 2016 by The Society of Dorset Men

A CIP catalogue record for this book is available from the British Library.

Paperback ISBN 978-0-9926594-3-1

Price £6.00

Printed in Great Britain by
Print Team (Dorset) Limited
www.printteam.co.uk

Contents

THE SOCIETY OF DORSET MEN

FOUNDED JULY 7th, 1904

'A Silver Tower Dorset Red Banner Bears'

President:
LORD FELLOWES OF WEST STAFFORD, DL

Deputy Presidents:
SIR ANTHONY JOLLIFFE, GBE, DL, D.Sc, D.Mus
DR. PAUL ATTERBURY, B.A. FRSA

Past Presidents:
SIR FREDERICK TREVES, BART, GCVO, CB, LLD, 1904 - 1907
THOMAS HARDY, OM, LITT.D, JP, 1907 - 1909
COLONEL JOHN MOUNT BATTEN, CB, 1909 - 1911
COLONEL SIR ROBERT WILLIAMS, BART, VD, 1911 - 1913
SIR STEPHEN COLLINS, JP, 1913 - 1915
JOHN CASTLEMAN SWINBURNE-HANHAM, JP, 1915 - 1919
THE RIGHT HON. The EARL of SHAFTESBURY, KP, PC, GCVO, 1919 - 1922, 1924 - 1925
CAPTAIN THE RIGHT HON. F. E. GUEST, CBE, DSO, 1922 - 1924
CAPTAIN ANGUS V. HAMBRO, DL, JP, 1925-33, 1936 - 1944
LIEUT.-COL. SIR PHILIP COLFOX, BART, MC, 1933 - 1936
H.E. THE RIGHT HON. LORD LLEWELLIN, CBE, MC, TD, DL, 1944 - 1957
BRIGADIER G. M. B. PORTMAN, CB, TD, DL, 1957 - 1961
ROBERT TOM WARREN, 1962 - 1963
COLONEL SIR RICHARD GLYN, BART, OBE, TD, DL, 1964 - 1969
SIMON WINGFIELD DIGBY, MA, TD, DL, 1970 - 1984
SIR ANTHONY JOLLIFFE, GBE, DL, D.Sc, D.Mus, 1984 - 2011

Past Hon. Secretaries:
WILLIAM WATKINS, JP, 1904 - 1925
H. LL. WATKINS, 1925 - 1937
S . H. J. DUNN, 1937 - 1940
E. G. GALE, 1940 - 1941
HARRY J. HARVEY, 1941 - 1942
F. C. H. DENNETT, AACCA, FRES, 1942 - 1961
W. T. G. PERROTT, MIWO, 1961 - 1969
J. C. R. PREWER, 1969 - 1979
G. E. HINE, FRICS, 1979 - 2004

Past Hon. Editors:
SIR NEWMAN FLOWER, 1914 - 1920
STANLEY L. GALPIN, 1920 - 1932
H. LL. WATKINS, 1935 - 1937
ASHLEY C. ROGERS, 1937 - 1950
FRANK C. H. DENNETT, 1951 - 1960
N. J. ('NAT') BYLES, 1961 - 1978
FRED LANGFORD, 1979 - 1994
GEORGE LANNING, 1995 - 2000
PETER PITMAN, 2001 - 2013
TREVOR VACHER-DEAN, 2014 - 2015

Foreword by Lord Fellowes

THE Society of Dorset Men, like any human organisation, has developed and changed over the years. As any reader may know, when the distinguished surgeon, Sir Frederick Treves, Bt., together with Lord Portman and other Dorset men of different degree, held the first meeting on the 2nd December 1904 at the Inns of Court Hotel, London, their desire was that those men of Dorset who were working in London should not lose touch with their native county, and that friendship should flourish between the Dorset-born residents of the capital. Now, we could be said to have a different goal, which is rather to investigate and proclaim the splendours and interests that make Dorset both a remarkable place to visit and a wonderful place to live, and the Society has re-located to the county, itself. But there is a common purpose, even so, which links us to the Society's past and that is to enjoy the many virtues and assets of the county and to allow the world to see how fortunate we believe we are to be Dorset Men (and women, of course).

I note that, in that first discussion when the Society was born, a Mr Taylor Hallett complained that Dorset was overlooked and, as a county with so much to offer, it should not be left out in the cold. A Mr Montefiore-Brice apparently agreed, observing that the railways had developed the seaside resorts of Devon and Cornwall but passed over those of Dorset. By contrast, I would think that our generation would attribute a good deal of Dorset's unique charm to the fact that it is rather off the beaten track. The lack of a motorway in the county, the entire absence of inter-city trains, have preserved an atmosphere that is out-of-the-way and, for most of us, worth the journey to taste. It is something of a miracle that has allowed Dorset to remain so unspoilt and I feel strongly that it is one of our chief imperatives, as modern residents, to stop its being spoiled now and rather to protect it for our children.

I was tremendously flattered to be approached by the late Roy Adams, a champion of Dorset if ever there was one, to see if I might accept the post as President of the Society. I knew I would be following in large footsteps. I was already familiar with Sir Frederick Treves, a pioneer of the reorganisation of field hospitals in the First World War and of course more famous to my generation for his work with John Merrick, the original Elephant Man, whom Treves rescued from a life of hideous degradation, providing him with a comfortable refuge for his remaining days. The film, starring Anthony Hopkins as Treves and John Hurt as Merrick is one of my most vivid memories. That a man as talented and imaginative as this should have been the founding President of the Society only added to its fascination. But he was followed by remarkable men in a more or less unbroken stream, with many ancient Dorset names among them, Digby, Ashley Cooper, Portman, Hanham, Glyn and many others. It seemed a challenge, not least to follow the marvellous leadership of Sir Anthony Jolliffe, new to the county as I then was, but I am heartily glad I picked up the gauntlet.

I am delighted that this account of the Society has now been written, still in time to catch much of its living history and to hear from the sons and daughters, grandsons and granddaughters, of the founder members. There is a good deal of fascinating detail to be explored, and what pleases me most is that there is throughout the strong sense that this Society, unlike many others, has always been for all the people of Dorset. Other elements may separate them, but when it comes to the love of the county they dwell in, they are united in their enthusiasm.

That truly seems to me to be something to celebrate.

Fellowes of West Stafford

The Lord Fellowes of West Stafford, DL, President of the Society of Dorset Men

Lord Fellowes of West Stafford, the President of the Society

Lord Fellowes succeeded Sir Anthony Jolliffe as President
of the Society in October 2011.

Julian Fellowes was educated at Ampleforth College and then at Magdalen College, Cambridge. He studied at the Webber Douglas Academy of Dramatic Art at South Kensington, London, and has pursued a successful career as an actor and writer for the stage, films and television as well as being a novelist. He was awarded an Oscar for the film Gosford Park in 2001, and has won several further awards, in particular for his highly successful television series, Downton Abbey.

As well as being the President of the Society of Dorset Men, he is Chairman of the Royal National Institute for the Blind Talking Books Appeal, Vice-President of the Weldmar Hospice Trust, and President of the Thomas Hardy Society. He was appointed a Deputy Lieutenant for the county of Dorset in 2008, and became a Life Peer in 2010.

The Beginnings

THE Society had its beginnings in the combined initiatives of two people, William Watkins and G. R. Crickmay (who was the architect of the Dorset County Museum and the former Dorset County Hospital.) In 1898 Crickmay organised a dinner and meeting at the Whitehall Rooms in London to promote the idea of forming the present Society. The meeting to form the Society was held on 7 July 1904 in the office of William Watkins at 62 London Wall. Letters of support were received from Thomas Hardy and the Editor of the Dorset County Chronicle, Ernest Young. The objects of the Society were set out as 'to establish a feeling of brotherhood between Dorset Men residing in or visiting London, to improve their knowledge of their native county, to assist members and their families who were in necessity, and generally to do all they could to help one another.' At this meeting William Watkins read an extract from a sermon by William Wake at a general meeting 'of Gentlemen and others of the County of Dorset: in the Church of St. Mary le Bow, December the 2nd 1690.'

Mr. W. WATKINS
(Honorary Secretary)

William Watkins
(1863 -1925)

WILLIAM Watkins was the founder-secretary of the present Society. He was born in Welshpool in Wales, and moved to Dorchester as a boy. He worked first as a solicitor's clerk, but then was invited by Sir Robert Edgecumbe to become the Company Secretary of the Baltis Land Company in London, where he was asked to form the Society of Dorset Men in London in 1904. Watkins was a close friend of Thomas Hardy who, with his wife Florence, attended Watkins burial in the Weymouth Avenue cemetery in 1925.

Archbishop William Wake (1657-1737)

WILLIAM Wake was born in Blandford Forum. After attending the Blandford Free School he studied at Christ Church, Oxford. He was ordained in 1681. From 1682 to1685 he was chaplain for the embassy in Paris. In 1688 he became preacher at Gray's Inn, a canon of Christ Church Oxford and a royal chaplain to William III and Queen Mary. In 1693 he was appointed Rector of St. James's, Westminster, and in 1703 Dean of Exeter. In 1705 he became bishop of Lincoln and then Archbishop of Canterbury in 1716. He was a controversialist and a noted church historian, writing a defence of the orders of the Church of England, his State of the Church and Clergy of England Historically Deduced published in 1703, continued to be regarded as the definitive account of English synods until the middle of the twentieth century.

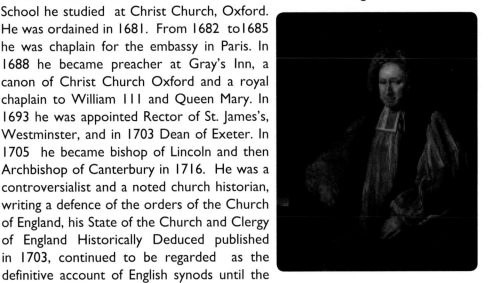

A copy of the front page of the sermon preached by William Wake, to the 'Gentlemen and others of the County of Dorset' assembled for their Annual Feast in December 1690. Wake refers to the event as a revival, 'After so long a discontinuance of these Friendly Meetings' which suggests that he remembered earlier regular meetings of Dorset men in London.

A SERMON
Preached at the Reviving of the
GENERAL MEETINGS
of the
GENTLEMEN AND OTHERS OF THE COUNTY OF
DORSET; IN THE CHURCH of ST. MARY le-
BOW. Decemb. the 2d. 1690.

By WILLIAM WAKE, D.D., Chaplain in Ordinary to
Their MAJESTIES, and Preacher to the Honourable
Society of GRAY'S-Inn.

To my Honoured Friends and Countrymen,

	Robert Norris		Thomas Castle
	Roger Hazard		Nich. Purchas
Mr.	John Dutton	Mr.	George Bisson
	William Oliver		Thomas Petty
	Henry Hillyard		John Cave
	Robert Colmer		John Ernle

Stewards of the Dorsetshire-Feast.

Gentlemen,

After so long a discontinuance of these Friendly Meetings, it could not but be a more than ordinary satisfaction
to me, to see them again revived in such times as these,
in which the Spirit of Christian Charity seems almost to
have been utterly departed from among us.

1 John, iv. 21.

"And this commandment have we from Him, That he
who loveth God, love his brother also."

Mr. WOODLAND and Mr. LEGG also spoke in favour of the
resolution.

THE first Annual General Meeting was held on 2nd December, 1904, when it was reported that 125 men had joined the Society which was to be known as "The Society of Dorset Men in London". The distinguished surgeon Sir Frederick Treves was elected as the first President and William Watkins was elected Secretary.

Sir Frederick Treves (1853-1923)

TREVES was elected as the first President of the Society. He was born in South Street, Dorchester, where he attended the school of William Barnes. He became a professor at the Royal College of Surgeons and a founder of the British Red Cross Society. He cared for Joseph Merrick, the 'Elephant Man' at the London Hospital, and was knighted for saving the life of the King, Edward VII, when he operated on him to remove his appendix two days before his coronation was due to take place in 1902. Treves visited every part of Dorset for his famous guide to the county The Highways and Byways of Dorset which was published in 1906.

A page of London Gazette advertising the 'Annual Feast for the County of Dorset' to be held at the Merchant Taylors Hall, in Threadneedle Street, London, on the 8th. of December 1693.

THe Annual Feast for the County of DORSET, will be held at Merchant-Taylors-Hall in Threadneedle-street, London, on the 8th of December inftant. Tickets may be had at Garraways Coffee-houfe near the Exchange, at Mr. Biffons at St. Pauls head in the Old Change, at Mr. Baxters Engraver, within the Middle Temple-Gate, at Mr. Dunfords at the 7 Stars at the Corner of Katherine-ftreet in the Strand.

A party of men from Weymouth are recorded as having dined at Greenwich in the middle of the 17th. century 'at a cost of twelve pence a head.'

The Society's Flag

THE design of the flag is based on the description given in a poem written by Michael Drayton in 1605 of the banner carried by the men of Dorset at the battle of Agincourt in 1415; 'A silver tower Dorset's red banner bears.'

This is a new flag, since the Society's original flag, designed in 1908, which was used to drape the coffins of both Treves and Watkins at their funerals in Dorchester, can no longer be found.

A fifteenth century illustration of the Battle of Agincourt

The Original Society Badge

THE Society's badge and motto were adopted by the committee on 28 February, 1908. Sir Robert Edgecumbe who had done the research for the banner and the badge had read a paper to the Dorset Field Club in November 1896, on 'The Arms of Dorchester and Dorset.' In this paper he referred to the book by the poet Michael Drayton on the Battle of Agincourt, and said that the Arms of Dorchester were certified by Clarencieux King-of-Arms in 1565 and quoted from Drayton's 1605 poem about the battle, 'a silver tower, Dorset's red banner bears'. Edgcumbe said 'So Clarencieux certifies for Dorchester in 1565 the Arms of the Dorset banner as borne at Agincourt, but...adding the shield of royal Arms...marking the fact that Dorchester was then a royal manor.' The report of Edgecumbe's lecture in the County Chronicle (26 November 1896) led to considerable debate, some correspondence arguing that Clarencieux refers only to the seal and not to the Arms.

Photo of the members of the committee in 1908 wearing the Society's badge.
William Watkins, Secretary and J. C. Swinborne-Hanham, J.P. Chairman,
seated in the front row

(1908/9 Year Book p.80-86)

The Society's Motto

THE Society's inaugural dinner was held at the Trocadero, on 27 February, 1905, and attended by some two-hundred and thirty members. The dinner was presided over by Sir Frederick Treves, who in his address quoted King Charles 11, who on coming to Dorset from Plymouth had said that 'he had seen no finer country either in England or out of it.' The members of the committee all wore distinguishing rosettes of white satin with red centres. A distinctly Dorset menu consisted of Portland mutton, Dorset apple cake, watercress, cider and Blue Vinney.

Among those unable to be present who sent greetings were the Bishop of Durham, Doctor Handley Moule, who enclosed ten guineas. In response to this act of generosity he was made a life member. Thomas Hardy, who had accepted the Society's invitation to be a vice-president, wrote in his letter, 'It is a sign of the times that modest little Dorset ...should at last have the courage to stand up to great London and say "Who's Afraid?"' This quickly became re-spelt in dialect form as "Who's A'fear'd?" and accepted as the Society's motto. This became incorporated in the badge of the Society which was adopted by the committee in February 1908. During the years of the First World War, this motto came to be the slogan of defiance and courage for all those from Dorset who were serving in every branch of the forces and in all the major fields of battle.

OUR MOTTO ILLUSTRATED (No. 4).

(By courtesy of "The Sketch" and the London Electrotype Agency, Ltd.)

When the Second World War began, the motto was blazoned across the front cover of the Society's Year Book in 1940, when the nation was confronting the threat of invasion.

" WHO'S A-FEAR'D P "

Among the guests at the Society's Annual "Veast" in May, 1950, was the Chairman of the Dorset County Council, Captain A.D. Pass. Responding to the toast, 'Dorset Our County' Captain Pass said that "he suspected the President of an ulterior motive when he invited him to respond. He probably expected him to apologise on behalf of the Dorset County Council, for their having appropriated the Society's motto without asking the Society's permission." He went on to explain that they had been one of the few counties in England which did not have an authorised coat-of-arms. A small committee was formed and adopted a new coat-of-arms but were unable to find a motto until one member declared that "there could only be one motto for Dorset, 'Who's A'fear'd?' "Somehow in the excitement of the moment we quite forgot that we had not obtained the consent of the Society of Dorset Men to use its proud motto...your President and the Society ultimately very kindly agreed that the County might share your motto." The motto has since appeared on all the County documents and publications, but it remains the property of this Society.

THOMAS HARDY, LL.D., J.P. (President).

Thomas Hardy

IN his Presidential address to the Society in 1908, Thomas Hardy imagined a young man from Dorchester arriving in London and his impressions of the city. Hardy lists the many Dorset connections with the capital, from the well-known fact of St. Paul's Cathedral being built from Portland stone, to the various historic associations through people from Dorset who established themselves in the city, which can still be traced by the number of places in London with Dorset names, such as; Weymouth Avenue, Dorset Square and Portland Place.

(REF. 1921 YR.BK.)

A copy of part of Hardy's handwritten presidential address to the Society in 1908.

1906: London Group visit to Dorchester and a welcome in the Borough Gardens

JUBILEE CLOCK
(Ref: 2007. p.113.
Art. & PHOTO
Borough Gardens

THE Society very soon organised outings to the home county for the London members which proved to be very popular. For their first visit on 15th. June, 1906, a special train brought a party of 250, which included sixty ladies, from Paddington to Dorchester West, where they were greeted by the Mayor, E.W. Young, the Editor of the County Chronicle. He led them immediately to the Borough Gardens, which were decorated for the main event which was the ceremony and presentation of the Jubilee Clock to the town as a gift from Society Member Charles Hansford. The band of the Warwickshire Regiment from Bovington Camp provided music for the occasion. They were then taken on a tour of the town by Harry Pouncy. This was followed by lunch as guests of the Mayor and Mrs. Young in a marquee which had been erected in the garden of Encombe, their house in Prince of Wales Road. Among those present were the Mayors of Weymouth and Shaftesbury, and the Rev. W. Miles Barnes, the son of the poet. A letter of greeting was read from Thomas Hardy, and in his speech of thanks for the welcome and hospitality, the Society's Secretary, William Watkins, gave credit to the Mayor, councillor Young, for suggesting to him when he left Dorchester for London in 1895 that he should start the Society. Following the lunch, a long train of horse-drawn charabancs and brakes took the whole party on a tour to Puddletown, on the way passing Thomas Hardy's house, Max Gate, and Came Rectory, which had been the home of William Barnes. They visited the church at Bockhampton and Athelhampton Hall and gardens before returning to Dorchester for the train back to London.

Then, the same year, on September 15th. and 16th. 1906, the Society's Committee made a visit to Weymouth, travelling from Paddington in a special saloon provided by the Great Western Railway. After a stop at Wrackleford for tea at the invitation of Alfred Pope, who was a vice-president of the Society, the saloon was attached to the 6.30 express to Weymouth where a banquet was provided at the Hotel Burden. Among the guests were many officers of the channel fleet and their commander, Admiral Sir A. K. Wilson, V.C. whose "imposing collection of battleships" were anchored in the Portland Roads and were a major local attraction. In his speech proposing a toast to the army and navy, Dr. Palgrave said "When Weymouth people saw the magnificent vessels which had gathered in the Portland Roads, surely no words were needed...to make them realise we were prepared for War." The following day the party was taken on a tour of the ships before taking the train back

The Channel Fleet in Portland Harbour - 1906

to London.

Sir Stephen Collins M.P.

IN July, 1908, Sir Stephen Collins, the M.P. for Kennington, and a native of Swanage, invited members of the Society to visit his home town. A party of 200 travelled by special train from Waterloo to Swanage, which was decorated with flags for the occasion. Collins had moved to London when he was fourteen and had succeeded in establishing a business supplying Purbeck stone for the very many new developments and hotels and theatres then being built. Like Portland stone, the stone from Purbeck has long been used in London's buildings- including Westminster Abbey. Among the recent buildings Collins had provided the stone for were the Hotel Cecil, Hyde Park Corner, Whitehall Court, the New Gaiety Theatre, His Majesty's Theatre, The Carlton Hotel, Wyndham's Theatre, Salisbury House, London Wall Buildings and many others.

Photo by   Fred R. E. Curtis.

CHILDREN WELCOMING THE LONDON-DORSETS.

Photo by   Fred R. E. Curtis.

IN MARY BRIDGE MEADOW SOME OF THE PILGRIMS.

Photo by   Mr. H. T. Nobbs.

"GOD BLESS THE DEAR CHILDREN WHO JOINED IN THE SINGING,
THEY SET THE JOY-BELLS OF OUR HEARTS ALL A-RINGING!"

(Photos: Y.Bk. 1922 p.91 & 92. Swanage quarries)

SWANAGE QUARRIES.

"SERMONS IN STONES," AT SWANAGE.

The Society's Collect

Used in Service at St. Paul's - 21st February 1908

O merciful Father, who dost put into thy children's hearts the love of home and country, we thank thee for the beauty and joy with which thou hast surrounded our lives, and especially for thy blessings upon our county of Dorset. Grant us, we beseech thee, grace to return the love which thou hast shown us, by providing for one another in sickness and distress, by strengthening one another in faith and life, by working together for the health, peace and prosperity of our native land. Give thy blessing to our Society and to all its members, that the brotherhood which has begun in this world may be perfected in the world to come, through Jesus Christ our only Mediator and Redeemer. Amen.

THE RT. REV. JOHN WORDSWORTH, D.D., BISHOP OF SALISBURY, PREACHING THE SERMON.

On 21st February 1908, a service for the Society was held in St. Paul's Cathedral. The preacher was the Bishop of Salisbury, the Rt. Rev. Dr. John Wordsworth, who was a Dorset man and a member of the poet's family. In his sermon he said that the county 'represents a natural unit of population - the settlement of a tribe. It is not mere administrative division or shire.' A special collect for the Society, written for the occasion, was used in the service.

(Account of service in 1908/9 YBK. P.32-37)

Dorset Men Beyond the Seas

IN 1909 the Society's secretary, William Watkins and his wife, took a world tour, visiting South Africa, Australia, New Zealand and South America, and other places in the Empire and where his companies had business interests, making contact with ex-patriots from Dorset wherever they went. This aroused an interest in the Society and a request that those from the county living and working overseas should be able to belong to it. They then formed their own societies which were affiliated to the Society in London. At the Annual Dinner in June 1910, the toast 'Dorset Men beyond the seas' was given for the first time. Watkins reported that 'London membership was now 600 with 150 overseas' including members in the USA, Brazil, Canada, China, Fiji, India, Newfoundland, Australia, New Zealand and Africa. At the 9th Annual Dinner in May 1913, Watkins said that 'he hoped that they could establish a "homecoming" reception every five years for Dorset men overseas. Steamship companies had agreed to give reduced fares to Dorset men coming home in this way.' This plan was prevented by the outbreak of the First

New South Wales Society of Dorset Men and Women on the Steamship Lady Hampton, at Pearl Bay, Sydney.

DORSET MEN BEYOND THE SEAS.
The First Executive of the New South Wales Society of Dorset Men and Women,
SYDNEY, 1912-1913.

Note: The ship is flying
the Society's flag.

Stauding.—Leonard H. Lani (Hon. Treasurer), Arthur J. Hare (President), Thos. W. Warren (Vice-President), J. Scott Young, C. J. Hart, A. F. Carrington (Hon. Auditor), Sitting.—Miss L. Ward, Mrs. L. Hart, Hon. Hilda Glani, Mrs. Hare, Mrs. Allan Warren, Mrs. S. J. Ward, Mrs. H. Brierley, James Ward (Vice-President), Captain; Herbert Caines, Hon. Secretary (Vice-President of London Dorset Society). Edward Thorne (Hon. Assistant Secretary).

PHOTO OF THE EXECUTIVE OF
THE NEW SOUTH WALES SOCIETY,
SYDNEY 1912-1913

The overseas societies included
women from the start.

Masonic Lodge Formed

London Dorset Lodge, No. 3221.
Consecration Banquet at the Holborn Restaurant, London, March 7th, 1907.
Col. Wm. Watts, C.B., P.P.G.W. Dorset, W.M. in the Chair.

W.Bro.J.M.Hunt,S.D.   Bro.H.Morgan,Org.   Bro.G.Tolley,Stw. W.Bro.J.H.Crickmay,D.C.   W.Bro.J.C.Milledge,I.G.   W.Bro.G.Ridout,J.D.
(8th.W.M.)   (9th.W.M.)   (7th.W.M.)   (6th.W.M.)

W.Bro.J.C.Swinburne-Hanham,Treas.   W.Bro.F.Bascombe,S.W.   Col.W.Watts,C.B.   W.Bro.J.White,J.D. W.Bro.H.W.Parker,Sec.
(4th.W.M.)   (2nd.W.M.)   (3rd.W.M.)   (5th.W.M.)

Notice of the proposal to form a Masonic Lodge in connection
with the Dorset Men in London, November 30th. 1906.
Two photos of the committee and members at the consecration banquet
of the London Dorset Lodge, at the Holborn Restaurant, March 7th, 1907.

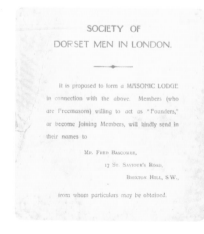

SOCIETY OF
DORSET MEN IN LONDON.

It is proposed to form a MASONIC LODGE
in connection with the above. Members (who
are Freemasons) willing to act as "Founders,"
or become Joining Members, will kindly send in
their names to

Mr. Fred Bascombe,

17 St. Saviour's Road,

Brixton Hill, S.W.,

from whom particulars may be obtained.

NAMES OF PROBABLE FOUNDERS

Brymer, Col. W. E.	Hounsell, F. A. K.
Bascombe, Fred.	Hunt, S. W.
Baskett, S. R.	Hunt, I. J.
Batty, C. H.	Huxtable, H. A.
Blake, R. S.	Milledge, J. O.
Burt, George.	Parker, H. W.
Case, Robt.	Pearce, Henry.
Crickmay, J. H.	Ridout, George.
Dominy, H.	Smith, W. J. Ham-
Foot, John.	Tolley, George.
Gerrard, A. W.	Vincent, Lt. Col.
Hanham, J. Swinburne-	Watts, Col. Wm., C.B.
Harvey, A.	White, John.

The Annual Veast

A short history by Hon. Sec. Hayne Russell

ALTHOUGH the first dinner, after the formation of The Society of Dorset Men in London, was held on 27th February 1905 at the Trocadero Restaurant in Piccadilly, there are known to have been at least two dinners previously organised for Dorset men living in London.

At the Merchant Taylor's Hall on 8th December 1692 a number enjoyed what was called an "Annual Feast", suggesting that this might have been held previously for a number of years.

In 1898 a dinner was held in the Whitehall Rooms with Lord Portman as Chairman, which was, in fact, the catalyst leading to the formation of the Society in 1904.

The inaugural dinner

In 1905 the company numbered 240, with Sir Frederick Treves in the Chair. As each member was introduced he shook hands. The menu consisted of dishes reminiscent of Dorset, such as Portland mutton, a Dorset pudding, Dorset watercress and Blue Vinny cheese. The order of proceedings for the evening set the pattern for all future dinners. These included the toasts "Dorset our County", "Dorset Men in London" and "Our Guests" with responses, a menu card which contained a number of dialect verses, the singing of "In Praise of Dorset" and eminent guest speakers.

At this dinner a letter from Thomas Hardy, who was unable to attend, was read out and included the phrase "Who's afraid ?" – later to become the Society motto "Who's a'fear'd?" The speakers were Mr. Clavell Slater KC , Mr. Fossett Lock - The Mayor of Camberwell, and Sir Frederick Treves. There was entertainment involving dialect poetry and music.

A "men only" event

Undoubtedly the success of the first dinner established a tradition and the second dinner was held on 19th February 1906, again at the Trocadero Restaurant. The bill of fare suggests that this was a feast of some proportion, consisting of a choice of two soups – clear pate d'Italie or thick St. Germain – a fish dish of boiled Ostend turbot, main course of boned sirloin of beef, a dessert of sweet Dorset pudding, followed by Pralinnee bombe and finally the Blue Vinny.

All the Dorset Mayors were invited and, although only four attended, this remained a tradition until the 1950s.

The third dinner saw a change of venue to the Holborn Restaurant and was held on Monday 6th May 1907 when 300 members attended. Comment was made in later reports on the physical task undertaken by Sir Frederick Treves to render a hearty handshake to everyone on arrival !

A presentation, of a silver tea and coffee service, was made to the Hon. Sec. William Watkins, who had been instrumental in the formation of the Society and in organising the dinners. A silver challenge cup was presented to Colonel Williams MP, to be competed for at the annual rifle meeting of the Dorset Volunteer Association. What happened to the cup remains a mystery.

A special distinction was given to the seventh dinner when, in response to the tribute of loyalty, a reply was received from the King. Given in Dorset dialect, as it always is, the tribute was sent by telegram prior to the proceedings and the reply received and read out later in the evening.

The tenth dinner on 4th May 1914 included an unusual entertainment in

The Society of Dorset Men in London.
Seventh Yearly Dinner, Holborn Restaurant, London, May 8th, 1911
The President, Colonel J. Mount Batten, C.B., in the Chair.

Dinners then continued to be held annually at the Holborn Restaurant although the sixth dinner, due to be held on 9th May 1910, was postponed because of the death of King Edward VII and, because of the hot weather and probable lack of refrigeration, it was not possible to obtain any Dorset Blue Vinny.

By now the dinners followed a set pattern and, because of the number of speakers and the entertainment, they must have made for very long evenings.

the form of a sword display performed by Lieutenant Wheeler of the Dorset Regiment.

Wartime and after

With the onset of the First World War the last dinner was held in 1915 and the Society reports stated "there were many who said it would be impossible to have a successful Dorset dinner in the middle of a war. Others declared the dinner was a necessity because at no other time had it been so imperative to keep the Dorset's calls for patriotism and support for those members serving in the forces. It was reported that a "Comforts Fund" had been set up to send gifts to men in the trenches and to those who were

Members of the Society of Dorset Men in London in the 2nd Batallion of the Dorset Regiment

prisoners of war in Germany. The Society had always maintained a close connection with the Dorset Regiment and the Commanding Officer of each battalion was an Honorary Member.

After the war the first dinner was known as "The Peace Dinner" and held at the Connaught Rooms on 5th May 1919. This was attended by several distinguished officers and amongst the speakers was Major General Sir Hugh Trenchard, later to be the first Air Chief Marshall of the fledgling Royal Air Force. Much praise was given to the exploits of the Dorset Regiment and the many members from "A'thirt the zeas" who had fought in the various campaigns of the war.

The London dinners continued as an annual feature in the Society calendar throughout the 1920s – held as near as possible to "Dorset Day", the first Monday in May. The Society flag always formed a backdrop with the County slogan "Vor Darzet dear the gie woone cheer" displayed above. The invitations, referred to as 'circulars' and sent to all members, were always in dialect and of some length.

Winston Churchill, one of the speakers at the 1924 dinner, having been detained in the House of Commons, arrived just as the Blue Vinny was being served.

Unfortunately there were vacant chairs at the 1926 dinner, specially organised to celebrate the Society's 21st year. The National Strike had prevented a number of members, especially from the County, from travelling. A special song was commissioned and sung at the event and for the first time the speeches were broadcast to the County by radio via Marconi's 2LO studio in The Strand.

Thomas Hardy never attended any of the dinners but did send his good wishes on a number of occasions in the early days.

One significant event of the 1930s was the vote taken at an extraordinary meeting of the Society on 28th April 1931 to simplify and shorten the title to The Society of Dorset Men. However the London dinners continued at the Holborn Restaurant. Reports are non existent for two years as no Dorset Year Books were published in 1933 and 1934.

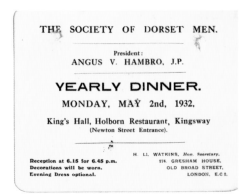

THE SOCIETY OF DORSET MEN.

President:
ANGUS V. HAMBRO, J.P.

YEARLY DINNER.

MONDAY, MAY 2nd, 1932,

King's Hall, Holborn Restaurant, Kingsway
(Newton Street Entrance).

Reception at 6.15 for 6.45 p.m.
Decorations will be worn.
Evening Dress optional.

H. Ll. WATKINS, *Hon. Secretary.*
274. GRESHAM HOUSE,
OLD BROAD STREET,
LONDON, E.C 2.

and seven of the eight county Mayors were present. In 1953 a Coronation Dinner was held and two of the speakers were from other County associations – the President of the Northumberland and Durham Society and the Chairman of the London Cornish Association.

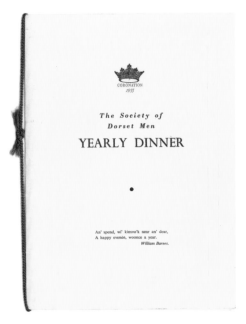

Throughout the remaining 1930s the dinners featured the Band of the Dorset Regiment, playing from the gallery in the King's Hall.

The last dinner, prior to the commencement of WW2, was on 28th April 1939. The committee decided at the AGM in October that the blackout regulations made it impossible to continue.

In May 1946, there was a small gathering of members in the Connaught Rooms in Great Queen Street, merely to commemorate the dinner date. The first Society dinner after the war was held in the Connaught Rooms on 5th May 1947. The Lord Chief Justice, Lord Goddard, was the main speaker and there was considerable consternation caused by a lack of Blue Vinny cheese because of rationing. It was back on the menu in 1949 when mention was made of organising functions "calculated to bring ladies into the picture". It was hoped that members would be supportive!

The 1950s

The new decade heralded another change of venue – this time to The Dorchester Hotel, Park Lane. In 1952 all the Members of Parliament for Dorset

The 50th anniversary of the founding of the Society was celebrated with a Golden Jubilee Dinner on 8th July 1954 and a special gold covered souvenir programme, including a history of the Society, was produced and signed by all those on "the top zettle" or top table. The President, Lord Llewellin, was unable to attend having been appointed Governor of the Federation of Northern Rhodesia, Southern Rhodesia and Nyasaland.

Another change of venue to St. Ermin's Hotel, Westminster was made in 1957 – also the year of a second yearly dinner; back in Dorset and at the Corn Exchange, Dorchester on 9th November.

Can ladies come too . . . ?

In the 1960s the London dinners continued to be held in May with the County dinner, now a permanent fixture, in November and moving to various venues around Dorset.

At the 1962 London dinner an extraordinary general meeting was announced to decide if Ladies should be admitted as members and invited to the London dinner. Both proposals failed but ladies were invited to the County dinner.

By 1970 numbers at the London dinner were down to around 60 – due, probably, to fewer members living in London and the growing popularity of the County dinner. Reports in the Dorset Year Book that had occupied six or more pages were reduced to two. Numbers of distinguished speakers were also reduced.

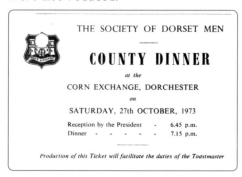

THE SOCIETY OF DORSET MEN

COUNTY DINNER

at the

CORN EXCHANGE, DORCHESTER

on

SATURDAY, 27th OCTOBER, 1973

Reception by the President - 6.45 p.m.
Dinner - - - - 7.15 p.m.

Production of this Ticket will facilitate the duties of the Toastmaster

It was mainly through the enthusiasm and efforts of Hon. Sec. Gordon Hine and Toastmaster Roy Adam, placing their stamp on both events for a number of years, that the dinners again became well attended. Whilst the Dorset dialect had always been an important feature of the dinners, Roy Adam brought his own special brand of humour to the fore at these gatherings.

It's the Lord Mayor's show

The 1983 London Dinner took place in the magnificent surroundings of The Mansion House Egyptian Hall in the City, at the invitation of the Lord Mayor of London, Sir Anthony Jolliffe. Three hundred members, and ladies for the first time, sat down to a meal of traditional Dorset fare, many having travelled up from Dorset for the occasion. Time honoured traditions were followed and Sir Anthony, in proposing the "Dorset Our County" toast said "I am proud to be the 655th Lord Mayor of London and the first to greet The Society of Dorset Men to the Mansion House."

At the 1984 dinner, held at Simpson's in the Strand, Sir Anthony Jolliffe was congratulated on his elevation from Lord Mayor of London to President of The Society of Dorset Men.

Throughout the 1980s two annual Society dinners continued to be held. As numbers at the London event diminished the County function became more successful with eminent speakers again being a feature. In 1986 amongst those attending were Lt. Col. Gerard Boucher, aged 90 and celebrating 50 years as a member, and Capt. R W Annand VC. The Guest of Honour in 1988 was the High Commissioner for Australia, the Hon. Douglas McClelland.

Farewell London – attention Dorset

In 1991 only 41 members attended the London Dinner and despite the report "that it was gratifying to receive continued steady support" it was to be the last. After 86 years, excepting the war years, the London Dinners

larger premises. After a trial period at Sherborne School the last three dinners have been held at The George Albert Hotel, just off the main A37 road between Dorchester and Yeovil, a popular venue that can seat 350.

came to an end. Yet the success and popularity of the Dorset event, usually held in October each year, has grown consistently.

On Saturday 3rd July 2004, to celebrate the centenary of the Society, 300 members and guests sat down to a four-course lunch amid the magnificent surroundings of the HQ Officer's Mess of the Royal Signals at Blandford Camp, in place of the usual County Dinner. The toast to "Dorset Our County" was proposed by Vice-Admiral Sir Barry Wilson KCB who, in a splendid speech, took the gathering through a history of the Society with special emphasis on the military and its exploits in Dorset. The President, Sir Anthony Jolliffe, responded and said "There will always be a Society of Dorset Men as long as there is a Dorset."

For several years the County Dinner was held at The Crown Hotel in Blandford but the ever growing popularity of the event meant finding

Distinguished guests

A major attraction always has been the important, and often very eminent, guests whom the President invited to be the chief speakers at the Dinner. During the early years in London, when the purpose of the Society was to re-connect with the county those who had left their native Dorset to make their homes and their livings in the city, the guests were usually those who had themselves been born in Dorset or had some strong connection with the county. So they would extol to those who had left them behind, the beauty of the countryside and the great attractions which Dorset possessed, to remind the members of their true home and stir their pride in belonging to such a special place.

Among the guests at the seventh Annual Dinner in May, 1911, was the colonel of the regiment, Lt. Col. Castleman-Smith. In his speech, just three years before the start of the First World War, he told the members that a small detachment of the Reserve Battalion would be at the coronation of George V and would also be in London for the unveiling of the Queen Victoria Memorial. He asked the Society to encourage the recruitment of volunteers as they were having difficulty keeping up their numbers. During the War, the guests were most often from the services, since the War was the subject most on people's minds, and many of the Dorset Men attended the Dinner in uniform, including the Society's Secretary, William Watkins, who had a commission in the National Guard. The chief guest at the Dinner in 1915 was Dr. Macnamara, the Parliamentary Secretary to the Admiralty, who replied to the toast of 'Our Sailors and Soldiers.' For Dorset Day in 1917, the Society held a Patriotic Concert at the Holborn, at which they received messages from Australian Dorsets, the Officer Commanding the 5th. Battalion of the BEF in France, and from Capt. H.O. Lock in India. The formal Dinner had been given up by this time for the duration of the War, and another concert was held the following year on Dorset Day in 1918, which was attended by over 300 men, most of whom 'were middle aged or in khaki.' The concert was to raise money to buy a band for the regiment, but the commander of the regiment, Col. Bullock, who was intending to be present, had just been killed.

The Dinner in May 1921 was attended by Corporal Jack Counter VC who had been made a Life Member of the Society. War heroes continued to be invited, and the Society was very pleased to welcome a particular hero to the Dorsets, Lt. General Sir Louis Bols, who was Colonel of the Regiment and had been their commanding officer who had led them to War in 1914 and was one of the most successful, admired and respected officers of the War.

In 1924 commenting on the number of guests from different parts of the Empire, Winston Churchill spoke about the importance of history and the British Empire "upon which…the best of the civilisation of the world depends."

Another famous guest in 1930 was the journalist and drama critic Hannen Swaffer. He told the company that he lived in a flat in the building where Thomas Hardy had lodged when he first began his life in London as an architect.

He said that he had been present at the first night at the Duke of York's Theatre when 'they sent to Dorset for a farmer's wife to play the part of Tess' which he described as 'a perfectly natural performance.' Having warned about English discoveries and inventions being neglected in England but taken up and developed by people in other countries, he said 'I do not want you to pay tribute to any foreign country, be English. Unless ideas continue to be spread in newspapers, in the theatre, in books, by films, by wireless (ideas which are ours) the next generation won't be English at all. Make your Society one of the local centres for the propagation of the best of English things.'

In May 1947 the Lord Chief Justice, Lord Goddard said that he was a Wiltshire, not a Dorset man, but knew Dorset well since he had spent many holidays in the county and had been for seven years the Recorder of Poole. Lord Hinchingbrooke raised concerns for the countryside which became an increasing theme in subsequent years. Saying, 'there is a task which confronts all the sons of Dorset in the coming year' he went on to speak about how much of the Dorset coast had been taken over by the War Office, warning that 'South Dorset is now being turned...into a military encampment – and the project will be backed up by all the military and commercial forces which come in its train...What is the use of a great standing army and fleets of aircraft if the source and inspiration of patriotism is lacking through the spoliation of our countryside?'

Among the guests at the Golden Jubilee Dinner were Sir Owen Morshead, Librarian to the Queen at Windsor Castle, and Ralph Wightman, a well-known writer and broadcaster on farming and the countryside who had been born in the Dorset village of Piddletrenthide. At the Diamond Jubilee Dinner in 1964, the main guest speaker was the Curator of the County Museum, Roger Peers, who spoke of his deep concern for the conservation of town and country in Dorset, quoting Thomas Sharp, whom he said was 'one of Britain's most influential planners.' Sharp had said of the English countryside, 'It is probably the most humanised landscape in the world; no other landscape has the friendliness of the English landscape, none its satisfying sense of serenity.' Sharp was one of those who daily warned that this country was being threatened by 'universal suburbia, vague, wasteful, formless, incoherent'. Peers went on to describe the spread of 'subtopia' on the 'outskirts of all our towns and many of our villages' saying that 'such is the pace of growth and change that the physical environment of this small island could be ruined by the end of this century.' Listing the destruction of ancient barrows and field systems, historic buildings and monuments, he concluded, 'The future of Dorset's heritage is in our hands. If we want to hand it down to our children's children we must work for it.'

This theme was taken up again the following year by the guest speaker, Lieut. Col. C. F. Linnitt, who in responding to the toast 'Dorset Our County' echoed Roger Peers, saying 'We must not allow the hillsides to be covered with pylons or our valleys to be disfigured with sporadic and piecemeal industrial development. Development must be done in such a away that the beauty of the countryside is not ruined or spoiled in any possible way.' This concern to protect the Dorset countryside and preserve it for future generations to enjoy continued to be expressed by speakers over the years, during which the Society's membership had been moving more into Dorset so that an autumn County Dinner had been introduced as well as the annual May Day Dinner in London. In 1980, Nicholas Baker MP., who spoke to the London gathering, said that his concern in Parliament was the Environment, with particular regard to development and tourism. He asked 'what sort of Dorset we wanted; we had to see employment was provided for young people, which the old agricultural industry used to do…The problem was to see that the environment in Dorset would still be beautiful in 20 or 30 years time.' The speaker at the County Dinner was the well-known television personality Jack Hargreaves who presented a regular programme about old country arts and crafts. In a forthright address he said 'When a city dweller saw an open space his first compulsion was to build on it… the countryside throughout the world would always be needed for food by the city dwellers. And so it was necessary to fight to preserve the countryside… It has been said that when God made Dorset, He then left instructions that it should be left alone.'

In May 1982, the President, Simon Wingfield Digby welcomed as the guest of honour, the Master of the Rolls, the Rt. Hon. Lord Denning, who spoke about his experiences as a Judge of Assize in Dorchester. The chief guest speaker at the County Dinner was the County Planning Officer, Alan Swindall. He warned the members that 'The past has rested fairly easily on Dorset, but I don't think the future will.' He spoke about the development in the east of Dorset, and said that further development was to be expected in oil exploration, in mineral exploitation and nuclear power. 'Its no good turning our back on these problems because it is by these that Dorset will contribute to the nation's well-being…At the same time we had a responsibility to guard our heritage…our task was to find the middle ground and relate the need for development with the desire for conservation.'

For the 200th. anniversary of the Battle of Trafalgar the Society welcomed a sailor, Captain Michael Fulford-Dobson, who spoke about Dorset's 'great contribution to the sea, providing countless generations of naval officers and sailors.' More recently the Society has welcomed the Lord Chief Justice of England and Wales, Lord Philips of Worth Matravers, the Lord Bishop of London, Dr. Richard Chartres, the Signal Officer-in-Chief of the British Army, Brigadier Ted Flint, Admiral Lord West of Spithead who was awarded the Distinguished Service Order for his part in the Falklands War, and the former chief of the Defence Staff, General Lord Guthrie of Craigiebank At the 2014 Dinner, the two speakers were Lt. General David Leakey, Gentleman Usher of the Black Rod - who told an entertaining story about getting stuck in the lift of the Victoria Tower of the Houses of Parliament with the Queen and the Duke of Edinburgh – and a fellow member of the Society, the well-known antiques expert, Dr. Paul Atterbury, who lives in Weymouth and said 'Weymouth is a place of such extraordinary potential, with the finest Regency seafront in England... I have become adopted by the county of Dorset and its rich history.' He praised the Dorset County Museum as 'one of the best regional museums in the U.K' and said 'Dorset is a magical county – people are very reluctant to leave – we don't realise how lucky we are.'

The President and guests at the 2009 Dinner with Admiral Lord West and General Lord Guthrie

The Society and the Thomas Hardy Players

THE Society was very supportive of the Dorchester group of amateur actors who presented stage versions of Hardy's novels and became known as the Thomas Hardy Players. In 1906, a well-known local lecturer and member of Dorchester Debating Society, Harry Pouncy, who was also a member of the Society of Dorset Men, presented an entertainment in the Dorchester Town Hall which he called 'A Dorset Day'. This included songs and scenes in dialect, and a stage presentation, "A Few Crusted Characters" performed by the members of the Debating Society. William Watkins then invited them to perform in London to the Society of Dorset Men. The first full play to be taken to London was "Far From the Madding Crowd" in 1909, where they attracted a great deal of interest in the London newspapers. Following this success, each of the productions by the Players was taken to London where they played to packed houses, and became nationally, and even internationally famous. The last of the plays to go to London was "The Famous Tragedy of the Queen of Cornwall" in 1923.

The Dorchester Debating and Dramatic Society in " The Mellstock Quire " (*in 1910*)

Photo : Wheeler Ltd., Weymouth

Back Row—Messrs. R. M. Dawes, W. H. Vine, A. Russell, H. C. A. Martin, T. H. Tilley, W. J. Fare (Prompter), and Mr. Smythe.
Second Row—Masters Stovey and Bugler, Mr. R. C. Barrow, Mrs. W. Major, Mr. L. L. Renwick, Mr. W. H. Jameson, Mrs. T. H. Tilley, Mr. C. R. Selley, Mr. H. Perham, Mr. T. Pouncy.
Third Row (seated) Miss M. Dawes, Mr. H. O. Lock, Miss Ethel Hawker, Mr. E. J. Stevens, Miss M. M. Hill, Mr. W. R. Bawler, Mrs. A. S. Hill.

WEST COUNTRY PLAYERS IN LONDON.

The Hardy Players photographed at Paddington on their arrival from Dorchester to-day. They are giving a performance of "A Desperate Remedy" at the National Sporting Club to-night. One wonders how they like London and its fog after the West Country.
"Evening News" Photograph.

William Watkins welcoming Gertrude Bugler as she arrives at Waterloo in January 1921 to perform in "The Return of the Native" for the Society in London.

The Dorset Year Book

EVERY year since 1904 the Society has produced The Dorset Year Book which is on sale to the general public. This contains articles contributed by members of the Society on every aspect of Dorset life, and is a remarkable record and valuable source of information about the history, folk memories and traditions of the county. The Society also produced a Newsletter to keep the members informed of all the Society's activities.

For those who had left Dorset to live overseas, the Society's Year Book was a welcome and much appreciated reminder of where they had come from. Some of them had been away from Dorset for a very many years and had extraordinary stories to tell. The 1915/16 year book reported the death in Sydney in August 1915, of Mrs. Joseph Kemp who had been born in Poole in 1817. She had emigrated to Australia with her husband in 1854, a journey which took 120 days. "Up to a few days of her decease…she could relate the starting of the railway in England and New South Wales, the old method of open voting in elections, the passing of the Reform Bill, the window tax, the corn laws, anti-slavery agitation etc… She was enthusiastic about Mr. Henniker Heaton's scheme for penny postage throughout the world. She remembered that it cost ninepence to send a letter from Poole to London." Another emigrant was Henry Facet Hurst, who had been born in Blandford in 1833. When he set sail for Australia in 1852, the ship stopped at Liverpool because the owners could not afford to continue the journey. The passengers then took over the ship themselves and continued on their way, taking six months to arrive at their destination. Hurst settled as a successful farmer, until his home was invaded by a notorious bushranger called Burke. In a fight to defend himself and his family, Hurst managed to defeat and capture the thief who was arrested, but sadly, Hurst died of the wounds he had received in the fight.

But the special appeal of the Year Book for those overseas, who eagerly welcomed the arrival of each issue, was in all that they could read in it about the county and the places they had come from and fondly remembered. The Society's President, Sir Frederick Treves, had travelled throughout Dorset in order to research for his book The Highways and Byways of Dorset which was published in 1906. He took nearly two thousand photographs of the towns, villages, and scenery all over the county, and he then gave these to the Editor of the Year Book, Newman Flower. So every Year Book was full of pictures of places which were very little changed from how they were remembered by those who had left them many years before.

How much receiving the Year Book meant to those in remote places overseas is shown by a letter to the Editor, dated December 12th. 1948, from Mrs. Gladys M. Stickland, with the address, c/o London Mission, Tientsin 1, N. China. Mrs. Stickland wrote: "Perhaps you and some of your co-workers on the Dorset Year Book would like to know how one copy of the 47-48 number reached its destination." She went on to explain that for eighteen months, she and two others from Britain had been in communist China carrying out medical missionary work. their mail from home arrived regularly at Tientsin, some ninety miles away and in order to receive it they depended on Chinese small traders who travelled to and fro to bring it to them. In September she had set out to go to Tientsin herself, intending to pick up the mail and also some hospital and household supplies. She describes the journey with a Chinese companion through fields of sunflowers and floodplains until they arrived at Tientsin. Having collected her supplies she then went to start the first forty miles of her return journey by train. Her journey was delayed and interrupted by officials frequently making her open all her bags for inspection "having everything dragged out and examined to see if it was what I said it was." After the third inspection she was ordered to go to a nearby village to see a V.I.P. He sent her back in an open railway truck to Tientsin. She spent two weeks there vainly trying to get a military permit, but without success, so she set out again without one. This time she managed to make it to the border "but a mean little man in uniform…collected my fountain pen, hand torch, my little case of personal medicines containing my pet eye and nose drops etc. He also collected my parcel of Chinese books." Luckily he was not interested in her mail bag which she managed to keep intact until October when she arrived back at her mission station. "Amongst my own mail was the Dorset Year Book. It has been much enjoyed by the three of us here, one a Welsh woman, the other an English doctor born in Madagascar, and myself plain Darset. The book will be re-read many times…Many, many thanks for such a splendid issue.. the farther away I am from Dorset the more I value every link…Yours very sincerely, Gladys M. Stickland."

(1949/50 Y.B. p.166-8.)

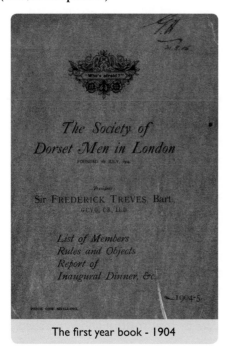

The first year book - 1904

Phone (01258) 820216

Tess' Cottage
Marnhull
STURMINSTER NEWTON
Dorset DT10 1NH

Mr Gordon Hine
Secretary, The Society of Dorset Men
Mortier House
New Road
SHAFTESBURY
Dorset SP7 8QL

4th December 1999

Dear Mr Hine

REPUBLICATION OF 1924 YEAR-BOOK COVER

Further to our telephone conversation earlier today, this is by way of a courtesy 'thank you' for your verbal agreement to the republication of the cover of the 1924 Dorset Year-Book. I hope to include it as part of an item for possible inclusion in a forthcoming 'millennium supplement' to The Marnhull Book, with which you are familiar.

As I told you, the cover of your publication, which shows a Marnhull cottage thought to be the setting for the family home in Hardy's Tess of the D'Urbervilles, adds considerably to the debate since it can by incontrovertibly dated and, most importantly, was published four years before Hardy's death -- and in the prestigious publication of a society of which Hardy himself had been a past president.

I am indebted to the sharp eyes of Dr James Gibson, a Vice-President of the Thomas Hardy Society, for bringing this connection to my attention. In due course I hope to be able to offer a copy of all of the material which I have collected with regard to this fascinating old building to both the Dorset County Record Office and the Dorset County Museum photo library.

Finally, I do hope you understood my reluctance to produce a piece for inclusion in your current journal. We are trying desperately to walk the fine line between being hospitable to the legions of Hardy enthusiasts who seek us out and not turning our private residence into a tourist venue, for which it is singularly unsuited -- we do not wish to draw any more public attention to ourselves than is absolutely necessary!

Thank you again for your help and kindness.

Yours sincerely,

Christopher Edwards

Copy to Dr James Gibson

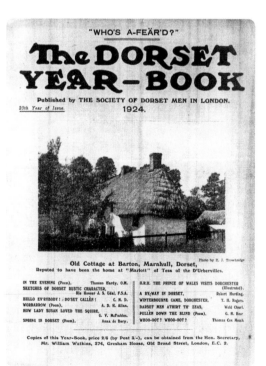

"WHO'S A-FEÄR'D?"

The DORSET YEAR-BOOK

Published by THE SOCIETY OF DORSET MEN IN LONDON.
20th Year of Issue.   1924.

Photo by E. J. Trowbridge

Old Cottage at Barton, Marnhull, Dorset,
Reputed to have been the home at "Marlott" of Tess of the D'Urbervilles.

IN THE EVENING (Poem), Thomas Hardy, O.M.	H.R.H. THE PRINCE OF WALES VISITS DORCHESTER (Illustrated).
SKETCHES OF DORSET RUSTIC CHARACTER, His Honour J. S. Udal, F.S.A.	A BY-WAY IN DORSET, Robert Harding.
HULLO EVRYBODY! : DO'SET CALLER! C. N. D.	WINTERBOURNE CAME, DORCHESTER, T. H. Rogers.
WOBBARROW (Poem), A. D. H. Allan.	DORSET MEN ATHIRT TH' ZEAS, Weld Charl.
HOW LADY SUSAN LOVED THE SQUIRE, G. V. McFadden.	PULLEN DOWN THE BLIND (Poem), G. H. Baur.
SPRING IN DORSET (Poem), Anna de Bary.	WHOO-OOT? WHOO-OOT? Thomas Cox Heath.

Copies of this Year-Book, price 2/6 (by Post 3/-), can be obtained from the Hon. Secretary, Mr. William Watkins, 274, Gresham House, Old Broad Street, London, E.C. 2.

Dorset Dialect

FROM the very beginning the Society has encouraged the use of dialect in a number of ways and has tried to ensure that it is not lost to future generations.   In almost every Year Book there has been articles, poems and stories written in dialect and has been part of the traditions which feature at many of the dinners.   For example, the welcoming of the Blue Vinny cheese accompanied by a dialect verse and the invitation to the annual dinner in London sent to all members until the early 1920's. The following is a part of the invitation from the Hon Sec William Watkins sent out for the 1914 dinner.

"Dear Zur

I do greet 'ee kindly, an' be in hopes that bist well an' 'arty!

I be martel pleased to tell 'ee that our girt Yearly Veast 'ull be 'eld agin theas year, an' avorfe th' Tenth ov Axen, in the Kings Hall o' the Holborn Restaurant, on th' Vourth Day o' th' merry month o' May.

We be now, look zee, in double figgers, an' to keep it up praper-like, we be in mind to 'ave a bright merry time o' it.   Zoo come along, an' don,t bide about on th' broad, or when thou com'st, thou midst vind thy pleace a-took, vor which I should be ter'ble zorry." and much more in a similar vein.

Another feature in the early Year Books was a long dialect article by Charles Rogers known as "Wold Charl" which was aimed at overseas members and conveyed news and items from the County.   Here is a short part from his 1922 offering.

,"On th' last day o' nineteen an' twenty-oone, I broke me journey down along Wimburn t' seek a laidy that liv'd sumwhere thereabouts, an' had a turk o' a job t' vind her.   Noobody sim'd t' 'av' yeard o' her - no, not even my good vriend Maister Charlie Frizzell, an' pon me honour there's not many roun' o' th' countryzide that 'ee doan't know.   Zoo I went on to Maister Hayter, th' chemist, t' ha' a little chow-chow wi' en ann' t' zeek his aid in vinden my vriend.   But as that prov'd a blank an' th' day was weren on, I was nigh-on gien up th' zearch when my vriend Charlie rush'd in like a bull in a china shop an' sed "Charl', I've vound her about a mile out o' town.   Wait a bit, an' I'll git me motor an' zide-car an' trundle 'ee auver"   Sake's alive! Ee did trundle me auver, an' at a perty vast pace too, in an' out th' traffic an' roun' carners like a zun-of-a-gun.   Shutten off th' injun, ee pull'd up at a cottage, an' th' door was open'd by a comely-lookin maiden avore I had time to knock.   "Cum in" she sed Muther sed smarnen she was sure as how Wold Charl was a-comin t'day"

Also, it was a tradition to render one of William Barnes poems "Praise o' Do'set" which had been set to music for the Society by Mr Boyton Smith at all the Annual Dinners.

We Do'set though we mid be hwomely

Bean't asheamed to own our pleace

An we've zome women not uncomely

Nor asheamed to show their feace

We've a mead or two wo'th mowen

We've an ox or two worth showen

In the village, at the tillage

Come along an' you shall find

That Do'set men, Do'set men, Do'set men

Don't sheame their kind

"Friends an' wife, fathers, mothers, sisters, brothers,

Happy, happy be their life !

Do'set dear, then gi'e woone cheer,

D'ye hear! Woone cheer"

MR. THOMAS HARDY celebrated his eighty-first birthday at Max Gate, Dorchester, on June 2nd, 1921. Our Society, through Mr. Watkins, sent the following message to their Past-President :—

"Th' Society o' Darset Men in Lon'on d' zend ee t'day their heart-velt good wishes, an' assure ee that, as the evenen shadders roun' ee gather, th' magic bond o' luv we've allus velt vor ee d' strangthen, an' your writens teake our mem'ries back t' th' fragrance o' a paist age, an' vill our hearts wi' jay. We be mindvul o' yer help in the early days o' th' Society, an' gratevul vor yer abiden interest in all our doens."

It is becoming increasingly rare to hear true Dorset dialect spoken as a matter of general conversation. Although, some words and sayings are still used by a few of the older generation in rural Dorset. However, the Society will continue to inspire its use where ever possible.

Charles Rogers, Printer and Publisher

Photo by C. R. Stride

Wold Charl tellèn Gaffer Clarke teäles o' the long ago.

CHARLES Rogers was one of the original group who had met together in the office of William Watkins in July, 1904, to form the new Society. He was born in Dorchester in 1860 and trained as a printer in the printing works of the Dorset County Chronicle. Aged 19, he left to go to London, where with his brother he was employed as a printer in Fetter Lane before setting up his own business as the Dorset Printing Works in the Waterloo Road, which was where the Society's Year Book was produced. He was a member of the first committee and served on the sub-committees for the entertainments, the annual dinner and the benevolent fund. He was also one of the first members of the London Dorset Lodge. He was fluent in the Dorset dialect in which he wrote many articles for the Year Book and regularly produced circulars in dialect for the Society which were often quoted in the London newspapers. When he died in 1931, he was buried in the Battersea cemetery at Morden, and his coffin was draped with the Society's flag which had previously been used at the funerals of the founder Secretary and the founder President, William Watkins and Frederick Treves. In 1934 a large granite memorial was unveiled to him bearing the Society's arms and motto "Who's A-fear'd?".

MR. STANLEY I. GALPIN.

A Foundation Member.

Mr. Galpin, in unveiling the Memorial said: " Fellow Dorsets and other friends of dear ' Wold Charl.' I would like first of all if I may, to thank Mr. Rogers' family for the great honour they have conferred upon me in asking me to unveil this Memorial. When our Society was formed in 1907, I had the pleasure of making the acquaintance of 'Wold Charl,' and that acquaintance, almost from the moment of meeting, turned into a friendship that lasted until the day he was unfortunately taken from us.

"I sincerely hope the friendship will be renewed in the life hereafter, when we hope again to meet him. I do not wish to take up your time, but I want to say this, that, although we laid his mortal remains beneath this memorial stone, we know that his soul and spirit rejoices, beyond the veil which our mortal eyes are not allowed to penetrate. We know he is there, and that he goes his way rejoicing. We are assured he is with us to-day, and I can almost hear his voice saying to us, ' Who's a-feär'd?' With all due reverence to the Glory of God, the Great Architect of the Universe, I now unviel this Memorial to the hallowed memory of dear ' Wold Charl.'"

Battersea Cemetery, Morden

The Memorial.

As the flag with which it had been enveloped fell to the base, there was revealed a monolith of grey Cornish granite, two tons weight, carved at the top with a cinerary urn and "Dorset's Red Banner," the Coat-of-Arms of the Society, emblazoned with the "Silver Tower," which is said to date from Agincourt, and bearing the familiar motto which Mr. Thomas Hardy chose for the Society.

The Memorial is a modified design from the drawing by H.E.C. Brickell of Portland.

In two centre panels are inscribed the following tribute and a dialect verse of G.H. Beer.

In ever loving memory of one who, through his own natural charm and his deep rooted love for the County that gave him birth, won a warm welcome in the hearts of all those who had the privilege of knowing him.

"Who's a-fear'd?"

"WOLD CHARL."

1860-1931

Erected by the Society of Dorset Men.

Sir Newman Flower

THE Editor of the Society's Year Book during the years 1914 to 1920, was a distinguished journalist and publisher, Sir Newman Flower. A frequent writer of articles and stories for the Year Book himself, through his publishing contacts he was able to obtain contributions, not only a regular poem from his friend Thomas Hardy, and considerable articles from Sir Frederick Treves, but also Sir Edmund Gosse, and writers as well-known as Warwick Deeping and the author of Three Men in a Boat, Jerome K. Jerome.

Newman Flower was born in the village of Fontmell Magna in 1879, 'then one of the loneliest spots in North Dorset.' Moving to London, he first worked on a penny weekly military paper, "The Regiment". In 1902 he joined the Harmsworth Press, and them moved to the publishers, Cassell and Company, rising to become its Chairman and President. Cassells was an old established firm, founded by a Manchester carpenter, John Cassell, in 1836. It developed as an educational publisher, producing Cassell's Popular Educator, and self-help books on history and art. Newman Flower was instrumental in building the company's reputation as their list of authors grew to include G.K. Chesterton, H.G. Wells, Arnold Bennett, and

Sir Newman Flower

such great public figures as Jellicoe, Asquith, Hindenburg and Winston Churchill, producing his monumental History of the Second World War. A considerable writer himself, and with a knowledgeable love of music, he wrote biographies of Handel, Sir Arthur Sullivan, and Schubert, and edited the Journals of Arnold Bennett. He was knighted in 1938. When he died in March 1964, aged 85, a memorial service was held for him in St. Paul's Cathedral.

(YB. 1964-5, p.49f.)

An Address on Dorset Butter

by Mr. John Foot, 17 March 1911

ON 17th. March, 1911, a lecture was given to the Society by Mr. John Foot, on the adverse effects of the Sale of Food and Drugs Act (1895) in "ousting Dorset Butter

The Society of Dorset Men in London.

President: **COLONEL JOHN MOUNT BATTEN, C.B.**
(His Majesty's Lieutenant for the Counties of Dorset and Poole.)

Past-Presidents:—
Sir FREDERICK TREVES, Bart., G.C.V.O., C.B., LL.D. (1904-5, 1905-6, 1906-7).
THOMAS HARDY, LL.D., J.P. (1907-8, 1908-9).

Chairman of Committee: Hon. Treasurer:
J. C. SWINBURNE-HANHAM, J.P.   Lord WOLVERTON.

Bankers: Deputy Hon. Treasurer: Hon. Secretary:
GLYN, MILLS, CURRIE & Co.,   JEROME BANKES, F.S.A.,   WILLIAM WATKINS, F.R.G.S.,
67, Lombard Street, E.C.   65, Redcliffe Gardens, S.W.   62, London Wall, E.C.

Telephone: 10345 CENTRAL.   **62, LONDON WALL,**
Telegrams: "DURNOVARIA, LONDON."   **LONDON, E.C.**

9th March, 1911.

DEAR SIR,

I have the pleasure to inform you that **Mr. John Foot,** a Member of our Committee, who is the Superintendent of the Public Health Department for the Metropolitan Borough of Bethnal Green, and an Associate Member of the Royal Institute of Public Health, &c., will read a paper at the **Holborn Restaurant,** on Friday, the **17th** instant, at **7.45** for **8** p.m., entitled :—

> "**Some anomalies of the sale of Food and Drug Acts and
> how they have assisted in ousting Dorset Butter
> from the Premier Position.**"

It is hoped that some representatives from the various Farmer's Clubs in the County will be present, and take part in the discussion which will follow.

Captain the Hon. Frederick E. Guest, M.P., will preside.

I enclose herewith Ticket of Admission for two.

Yours faithfully,

WILLIAM WATKINS,
Hon. Secretary.

FIXTURES.

Tuesday, April 4th ... Bohemian Concert, Holborn Restaurant.

Monday, May 8th ... Yearly Dinner, Holborn Restaurant.

from its Premier Position".   Foot was the Superintendent of the Public Health Department of Bethnal Green and had been on royal commissions and enquiries into the sale of food and drugs. Talking about the adulteration of food (which he said was the responsibility of the wholesaler and not the retailer) he referred to the "sale of a mysterious product known as butterine" and said that "Three judges of the High Court…professed themselves quite unable to say precisely what was meant by the word butter."

Thirty years before, Dorset butter had set the standard for "fixing the price and position of every other brand." But the sale of butter substitutes and the active market of Danish butter in England had "deposed from first place" one of the county's staple products. "It was not fair competition that defeated best Dorset in the markets. Rather it was competition of a most unscrupulous character that had enabled foreign butter and butter substitutes to flood the markets."

A SONG OF FOUR COUNTIES

by Stanley Galpin and A Kingston-Stewart

Dorset gives us butter and cheese

Devonshire gives us cream

Zummerzet's zyder's zure to please

The heart of a rural Dean;

Cornwall from her inmost soul,

Brings tin for the use of man,

And the four of them breed the prettiest girls,

So damme beat that if you can!

The Society and the Military

Pride, Caring and Response

FROM the beginning, the association between the Society and the Dorset military has always been close. The story of the regiment from its first forming in the 18th century is an integral part of the proud history of the county. The Society was quick to recognise this, and the commanding officers of the regiment were appointed honorary members of the Society. At the third Annual Dinner in May, 1907, the Society presented Colonel Williams, the commanding officer of the 1st. Volunteer Brigade of the Dorset Regiment, with a silver challenge cup to be awarded annually to the winner of a rifle shooting competition. The first contest took place at the Bovington Range in June 1907 which was won by Sergeant S. Green of Gillingham. He went on to win four years in a row, so at the 7th. Annual Dinner in 1911, the Society presented him with a replica of the cup . In March, 1907, Colonel William Watts became the first Worshipful Master of the newly formed Dorset London Lodge of Freemasons. The Annual General Meeting in November, 1909, elected the Lord Lieutenant of Dorset, Colonel John Mount Batten, to succeed Thomas Hardy as the Society's third President.

Photo by   Goodfellow, Gillingham.

SERGEANT S. GREEN.

Silver Challenge Cup presented to the Dorset Volunteer Association.

In his address at the Annual Dinner in May that year, Colonel Mount Batten had spoken about the current strength of the Territorials, asking the Society to encourage more young men to join, and told the Society that the King was going to present them with new colours at Windsor Castle in June. At the Annual General Meeting in November, 1911, the Society elected as its fourth President, Colonel Sir Robert Williams, who was a director of the London and South Western Railway, and had previously commanded the Dorset Volunteers. In his Presidential address to the Annual dinner in May, 1912, he referred to the Regiment's motto 'Primus in Indis' which they had gained as the first British Regiment to be sent to India in 1751. The Society's Year Book published an account of the Dorset Regiment and some of its leading personalities, which included Major Wadeson V.C., Colonel Hambro and Colonel George Pleydell of Smedmore.

In 1914, just before the outbreak of the First World War, Colonel Sir William Watts gave a detailed lecture on the history of the Regiment to the Society in London. A full account of this lecture was printed in the Year Book for 1914/15. As the War continued the Society's relationship with the Regiment grew stronger and closer as those of the Members themselves who were in the forces or young enough, joined up and left for the various fields of battle. That year, the Year Book included its first 'Roll of Honour' which contained the names of ninety Members and the members of their families who were now in the War, among whom were eight members of the Pope family, the well known Dorchester Brewers, all except one of them officers. The 'Scroll of Fame' in the same issue, gave accounts of the deaths of the son of the Society's vice-president, Mr. J. Shortland Aplin, and of Captain John Batten, the son of the Society's former President. The Annual General Meeting on 11th. November, 1914, began with sympathy for Colonel Mount Batten and his family, and reported that over £200. had been raised by members for the fund which the Society's Secretary, William Watkins had instituted to provide comforts for the men in the forces. Parcels of tobacco and chocolate had been sent to the

OFFICERS OF THE FIRST DORSET REGIMENT WHEN THE WAR BEGAN.

Back Row—LIEUT. A. K. D. GEORGE. CAPT. WHITE. CAPT. WILLS. LIEUT. WOODHOUSE.
Fourth Row—LIEUT. FRAZER. LIEUT. GRANT DALTON. LIEUT. GREGORY. LIEUT. SHANNON. CAPT. KITCHEN.
Third Row—LIEUT. BUTCHER.   LIEUT. LEISHMAN. LIEUT. CHUTTERBUCK. LIEUT. CLARK. LIEUT. TURNER. CAPT. MOULTON BARRETT

Second } LIEUT.   LIEUT.   CAPT. CAPT. AND QMR. LIEUT.   CAPT.   CAPT.   LIEUT.   LIEUT.   CAPT.   CAPT.
Row } BURNARD.   KING.   ROE.   GYNGELL. PARTRIDGE.   RATHBONE.   HYSLOP.   PITT.   HAWKINS.   PRIESTLY.   KELSALL.
Sitting—CAPT. WILLIAMS.   CAPT. FRASER.   MAJOR ROPER.   COL. BOLS, D.S.O.   MAJOR SAUNDERS   CAPT. DAVIDSON.   CAPT. AND ADJUTANT RAMSONE

Front, and an appeal had been made to wives and lady relatives to make mufflers, cardigan jackets, body belts, mittens and socks for Dorsets on active service. Watkins had already received a letter from the Front thanking the Society for the gifts. The Dorset Men Beyond the Seas had also become involved in the War. In New Zealand, within twenty minutes of the announcement having been made, on August 5th, that war had been declared, 400 men had reported for duty. The Penang Volunteers, commanded by Arthur Adams, a life-member of the Society, was the first irregular unit to be declared an imperial force.

Throughout the War, the Society was kept informed with what was happening to the Dorset Regiment and to all those from Dorset in the other services. Field-Marshall Sir Evelyn Wood, V.C. gave a lecture to the Society on 'The Dorset Regiment in War' which included historical references to the Monmouth Rebellion of 1685 and a fight with Baluchi robbers in India under Sir Charles Napier in 1845, but also came right up to date with an account of two battles on the 1st of May and the 13th of October, 1915, 'when a battalion of the regiment continued to fight determinedly...even after a loss of nearly fifty per cent.' Each year, as the war dragged on, with its terrible casualties, the Year Book featured articles about what those from the county had been doing. In the 1915/16 issue, the Year Book's Editor, Newman Flower, wrote a long account of 'What the Dorsets have done in the Great War', detailing the engagements in which the different battalions of the Regiment had been involved, which covered almost every area of the war, from Flanders, and Hill 60, where the Dorsets were the first to be attacked by poison gas, to Gallipoli, India, the Dardanelles and the Persian Gulf. In another article in the same issue, William Watkins, wrote an account of the comforts fund, which he said had received gifts of money from 'India, China, Africa, Australia, New Zealand, the Solomon Islands and many remote corners of the Empire...and also from American friends". Parcels were also sent to prisoners of war and the wounded in hospitals in England, who were visited by members who took comforts to them. Where possible, donations were raised to help the bereaved dependants of those who were killed in action. A notice was put up in every post office in Dorset which said that if anyone had wounded relatives brought to London the Society would arrange for them to be met when they arrived at any of the London stations to give them help.

It Meant So Much ...

The label here depicted - the original being printed with the crest in red and the printing in blue on white paper - was kindly loaned for reproduction by Lt.-Col. D. V. Wakely, M.C., (Retd.), Curator of the Dorset Military Museum. It was one of the gifts to the troops in The Dorset Regiment, provided from the war-time (1914 -18) "Comforts Fund" of the Society of Dorset Men in London, this particular one being from cigarettes received by Mr. Devine of Winchester when then aboard the Troopship S.S. Castalia with the 2nd Battalion en route for India.

Extract from the history of the Dorset Regiment 1914-18

APPENDIX I.

The Work of
The Society of Dorset Men in London,
1914-1918.

Shortly after the outbreak of war it was felt that the members of the Society would wish to contribute to the comforts of those gallant sons of Dorset who were serving in all parts of the Empire, both on land and sea.

The Society of Dorset Men in London therefore inaugurated a fund called " The Creature Comforts Fund," and with the help of its members and their friends were able to maintain this throughout the four long years of conflict.

On launching this appeal the immediate response was amazing, promises of help in money and kind simply poured in. Furthermore, the enthusiasm of the members to do all they possibly could for their fellow County-men and kindred never abated, and the Committee knew that so long as the need was there, the response would be forthcoming.

During the four years the Society raised in cash the sum of over £2,000. This amount was collected in various ways, many sending donations from themselves and their friends, others monthly subscriptions, while our oversea members were continually sending their gifts. Many concerts and entertainments were organised by members of the Committee and their friends, these at all times received the hearty support and co-operation of the members. On each and every occasion the services of the artistes were generously given and the proceeds from the sale of tickets and programmes considerably helped to swell the funds. These were expended to the very best advantage, the objective being to provide and send out a continuous supply of comforts to the Fighting Forces hailing from the County. The comforts took the form of :—

Tobacco, cigarettes, matches, chocolate, biscuits, peppermints, brandy-balls (from Shaftesbury), socks, shirts, gloves, mittens, helmets, body-belts, sleeping-socks, cardigan jackets, handkerchiefs, rolled bandages, scarves, note-paper and envelopes, soap, candles, copies of periodicals, playing-cards, games, footballs, football shirts, knickers, sweaters and boots, cricket bats, balls and stumps, while band instruments and music were sent out to the 1st Battalion, and mouth organs to the 2nd Battalion. Each Christmas an enormous supply of christmas puddings were despatched to the various units.

Parcels were also despatched by the Society to Prisoners of War, the wounded in hospitals in England, in fact parcels were sent to any part of the world wherever a Dorset soldier could be found. The wounded who were sent to hospitals in England were visited and cheered and some special creature comfort taken to them even if only a few " Woodbines."

It is not too much to say that the appeal to support the Creature Comforts Fund was most nobly responded to, and had it not been for this spirit, which was in such practical evidence the whole time, the Committee could not have carried out the work which was so much appreciated by our men.

Letters received from time to time from those in command, as well as from individuals, expressed great appreciation of our work and of all that it meant to those who were serving to know that they were not forgotten.

At the close, a handsome donation was made to the Earl of Shaftesbury's Fund to provide Silver Bugles and Drums for the Dorsetshire Regiment.

My Call to Dorset by Princess Catherine Radziwill

IN 1915, the Society received two letters

from the Princess Catherine Radziwill, 'a member of the Russian Royal family' which they published in the 1915-6 Year Book. Princess Catherine was born in 1858, and when she was fifteen she married Prince Wilhelm Radziwill, a member of an aristocratic Polish-Lithuanian family. In her first letter she writes about "how the war came to Russia" and "how the poor people... heard the voice of their beloved Tsar calling upon them to rise up and help him." She appeals to Dorset "Do your best, so long as there are young men in your land, and go and meet the enemy who is menacing you...Come Forward in your legions...I call upon you Dorset men to rise, and to pour more of your fine regiments into the fields of conflict in the name of all the poor Russian peasants who have given all they had..."

Her second letter, dated 29 October 1915, was addressed directly to the Editor of the Year Book, Newman Flower, and is a further appeal to the men of Dorset following the execution of Nurse Edith Cavell by a German firing squad in Belgium. Edith Cavell was a British nurse who was matron of a nursing school and clinic in Brussels which in 1914 was taken over by the Red Cross. After the city was occupied by the Germans she sheltered British and French soldiers and helped them to escape to Holland which was a neutral country. She believed it was her Christian duty as a nurse to save lives, but she was betrayed by a French man (later tried as a traitor by a French court.) She was held in solitary confinement and put on trial by the Germans who accused her of treason in violation of their military law. With complete honesty she admitted her guilt and signed a statement the day before her trial where she was sentenced to death. The night before she was executed she told the chaplain, "Patriotism is not enough, I must have no hatred or bitterness towards anyone." Her trial and sentence received world-wide publicity and

several appeals were made, especially from America, for the Germans to spare her life, but to no avail. She was shot by a firing squad on 12th October 1915. Her death resulted in a great deal of anger against the Germans who were condemned as brutal murderers, and added to the instances of German indifference to the sufferings of civilians which in particular, strongly influenced attitudes in the United States and eventually brought them into the war. In her letter, Princess Radziwill wrote "Tell this to your Dorset men…and bid

them never to forget Edith Cavell, nor her martyrdom which she endured for a cause which I feel sure they will be more eager now to defend than they even were before."

In 1919 a British naval ship brought Edith Cavell's body back to Britain for a national service in Westminster Abbey, it was then taken to Norwich where she was buried in Life's Green close to the Cathedral. Her national monument in London stands by St. Martin's Lane near Trafalgar Square.

(1915-6 Year Book ps. 23-5. & p.100)

The popular lecturer, Harry Pouncy, who before the war had given several lectures to the Society on Dorset customs and folk-lore, gave a lecture to the Society at the Holborn Restaurant on "The Great War and Dorset's Share in it." This event was chaired by Colonel Bols, DSO. who had commanded the regiment when it was first sent to France in August 1914. Evidence that the Society's concern for and efforts on behalf of the troops was being appreciated came on the day of the Annual Dinner in May, when in the Sergeants' Mess of the 2nd/4th. Dorset Regiment in India, the Company Sergeant-Major D.J. Fry, proposed the toast of "The Society of Dorset Men in London."

From the 1916/17 Year Book, until the end of the war, Harry Pouncy contributed articles on "the Dorsets in the Great War." In the first of these, referring to the 'Ubiquitous Dorsets', he describes 'the 1st. Dorsets…from Mons to the Marne', the 'doggedness' with which they hung on to the trenches at Govenchy, from the 12th to

the 15th of October, 1914. The Dorset Yeomanry under Lt. Col. Troyte-Bullock made a dismounted charge at Hill 70 in Gallipoli. The cavalry charge against the Senussi Arabs' machine guns at Agagia in Western Egypt, the 2nd. Dorsets in Mesopotamia, and General Gorringe's relief force 'which…failed to avert their catastrophic surrender through starvation at Kut-el-Amara.' He also gave

2nd. Batallion Dorset Regiment
Survivors of the Seige of Kut-el-Amara

Private J. Cole   Lance Corporal J. Wiliams
Brg. Q.M.S.F. Harvey   Reg. Sergeant-Major G. DeLara   C.O.M.S.R. Maidmont

accounts of the Dorset men in the navy and the Royal Flying Corps, saying that the cruiser HMS. Birmingham, which sank the first German submarine to be sunk in the war, on 9th August, 1914, was commanded by Captain Duff of Morton, and reporting that "The greatest loss that Dorset has suffered in the navy during this war has been Rear–Admiral the Hon. Horace Lambert Alexander Hood" who was killed when his flag-ship, Invincible, was sunk at Jutland.

Lieutenant-General Sir Louis Bols

MAJOR-GENERAL Sir Louis Bols was one of the most remarkable, successful and highly regarded commanding officers of the First World War, although he is not as famous and well-remembered as he deserves to be. The Times in its obituary said that his was 'A military career of exceptional distinction.' When the war began in 1914, he was a Lieutenant-Colonel, in command of the 1st. Battalion, the Dorset Regiment, which was among the very first to be sent to France. Four years later, he was a much decorated Major-General, and Chief of Staff to General Allenby in Palestine.

Jean Louis Bols was born on 23 November, 1867, in South Africa, the son of the Belgian Consul-General, and his English wife. With his family he travelled to his father's postings in Sydney, Budapest and Quebec before beginning his formal education at Lancing College in Sussex. In 1887 he was commissioned in the Devonshire Regiment and served in Burma and India. In 1898 he was on the India Station Staff, and then in 1899 became the Adjutant at Aldershot. Then, following the outbreak of the second South African war, he returned to the country of his birth, where he came under the influence General Sir Henry Hildyard, a leading moderniser and military strategist. During Hildyard's time as the Commanding Officer of the Staff College at Camberley, Generals Robertson and Allenby, and Field Marshall Haig had all studied under him, which meant that his teaching had an important influence on the conduct of the First World War.

In South Africa, Bols was in action at the battles of Colenso, Spion Kop and at the siege of Ladysmith. He was three times mentioned in despatches and awarded the DSO. and the Queen's and the King's medals. He returned to England and after attending the Staff College at Camberley, in 1905 he was in command of a company of cadets at the Sandhurst Royal Military College, where he was appreciated for 'his extraordinary tact and charm.' Then, in 1907, as a Brigade Major, he went to Germany where he attended German army manoeuvres. His report to the War Office contained a warning of the efficiency of German preparations for war. On his return he was appointed to the Staff College where it is reported that he was very popular. With the Dorset Regiment in France in 1914, he took part in some of the worst battles of the war, in Mons, Le Cateau and the Marne. He was offered a staff appointment but his corps commander refused to let him go. He commanded the Dorsets at Givenchy and Le Bassee, but then, in November 1914 he was wounded and captured by the Germans but managed to escape.

Returning to the Front he led the 15th. 13th and 84th brigades in turn at the battle of Ypres which cost the lives of 5,600 of his men out of his original 7,000. In 1915 he was appointed Brigadier-General on the general staff and a C.B. As Major-General on the general staff of the Third Army under General Allenby, Bols was responsible for planning operations for the battles of the Somme and of Arras. In a tribute to him, Allenby wrote 'his was the fertile brain to plan and prepare the Battle of Arras, which resulted in the greatest success achieved up to that date in the War.' Promoted again, he commanded the 24th Division at Messines Ridge in June 1917. The same month he became Chief of Staff to Allenby who was now leading the fight against the Turks in Palestine. There, "Bols showed his profound knowledge of the handling of troops, their limitations and their skilful use, which enabled him to effect one of the most brilliant feats of the War: the capture of Jerusalem and the final defeat of the Turks in Syria. " During this time he was mentioned in despatches twelve times and as the war came to an end he was appointed KCMG.

In 1919 he attended the Peace Conference in Paris, then returned to Palestine which the British held as a mandate, as the chief administrator. He continued his army career and his Dorset connection by becoming the Commanding Officer of the 43rd. Wessex Division and South West area in 1920, and Colonel of the Dorset Regiment and of the 12th. London Regiment in 1921. In 1928 he was appointed Governor of Bermuda. It

Major-General Sir Louis Bols, K.C.B., K.C.M.G., D.S.O.

was written of him that "as an executive officer he had few equals in the service. He was of kindly and sympathetic disposition, and possessed a keen sense of humour." He died at his home in Bath on 13th. September, 1930.

(Ref. Main sources, DNB. and Times obit.)

Lord Trenchard of Wolverton (1873-1956)

LORD Trenchard is remembered as the "Father of the R.A.F." In World War I as Commander of the Royal Flying Corps, he advocated the separation of air and army forces and was chiefly responsible for the establishment of the R.A.F. in 1918. He became the first Air Marshall and chief of the air staff. After the war in 1931 he became the commissioner of the Metropolitan Police and founded the police college at Hendon. Although he was born in Taunton in Somerset, he was a member of the old Dorset Trenchard family who built Wolfeton House just outside Dorchester.

He was a Vice-President of this Society and in May, 1921, was one of the main speakers at the annual Dorset Day Dinner. In his address he paid tribute to another Dorset man, Lieutenant William Rhodes-Moorhouse, of Parnham Manor, who had been the first member of the R.F.C. to be awarded the V.C. Moorhouse had been on a reconnaisance mission to spot the movement of German reserves at the second attack at Ypres. Although seriously wounded, he managed to return to his base and make his report. He landed safely, and received a message of commendation from the commanding officer, Lord French, on the success of his mission and expressing admiration for his courage and the way he had carried out his duty. Sadly, Moorhouse subsequently died of his wounds.

(Yearbook 1922 p.52 & 53).

Private Jack Counter V.C.

WHEN the members of the Society met in November 1919, for its first Annual General Meeting after the ending of the War, it was reported that the membership was the largest in its history due mostly to the number of service men who had joined following the Armistice. Among those who had returned was Private Jack Counter, who had been awarded the Victoria Cross. It was unanimously agreed that he should be made an honorary Life Member of the Society.

Jack Counter had been born in Blandford in 1898 and worked in the International Stores. He joined the army in 1917 and was sent to France with the 1st. Battalion of the King's Liverpool Regiment. On the 16th of April, 1918, his company were facing an enemy breakthrough at Boisleux St. Marc. A party was sent out to discover the size and number of the enemy troop placements opposing them but this failed. It was then thought that an individual soldier on his own might be more successful as being less likely to be spotted. But each of the first five men who tried this was killed. Jack Counter then volunteered, knowing well that his chances were no better – and even worse – than the others before him, since the enemy was now well aware of what was being attempted. In spite of the terrible danger he faced from the enemy fire, he was able to succeed in his mission and return with the vital information which enabled his commanding officer to launch a counter attack which recovered his regiment's position. Jack Counter then carried five messages across open country under heavy artillery barrage, to his Company Headquarters. His award of the Victoria Cross appeared in the London Gazette on 23rd. May 1918, and he received it from King George V at an investiture in Buckingham Palace. When he returned home to Blandford he was met at the station by the Mayor and the town band and was made an Honorary Freeman of the Borough. He was presented with a savings certificate and also a gold watch by his former employers. After the War he moved to the Channel Islands and worked for the Post Office. After he died in 1970 the Jersey Post Office marked the 50th. anniversary of the British Legion with a special Jack Counter V.C. stamp in his honour.

(Year Book refs: 1918-9 p.60. 1988 p.56.)

After the war ended, and the Society resumed its peace time activities, when the Committee met in 1919 its members felt that as 'During the War the Society was in constant touch with the Dorset units of the fighting service...this should not lapse now the War was over.' The army units themselves continued to provide reports for the Year Book with an article from Lt. Col. C.C. Hannay, the commander of the 1st. Battalion, saying that it had been re-formed in Dorchester in June 1919. At the the Annual General Meeting in November, 1919, the Earl of Shaftesbury, who had served in the war himself as the Brigadier-General commanding the 1st. South West Mounted Brigade, was elected President. It was reported that a letter had been received from Lt. Col. Radclyffe, the commander of the 2nd. Battalion recently sent to India, expressing enthusiasm for 'the liaison which exists between all ranks of the 2nd. Dorsets and the Society...the more we see of each other the better for us all.' The Society found practical ways of continuing the association as Lord Shaftesbury made his first appearance as the Society's President at a concert in February 1920, in the Steinway Hall, London, which was held in aid of a fund to provide drums and bugles for the regiment. These were obtained and presented to the regiment at a ceremony in May 1920, at the Depot Barracks in Dorchester. Then, at the Society's AGM. in November, William Watkins asked for help in providing employment for men of the Dorset Regiment 'of whom many... were constantly writing to him.'

Earl of Shaftesbury, K.P., K.C.V.O.

THE EARL OF SHAFTESBURY.

Photo. Bassano

THE Society's seventh and then ninth President was the distinguished ninth Earl of Shaftesbury, who was President twice, from 1919 to 1922 and then again in 1924-5. He was the grandson of the seventh Earl, the great social reformer, whose memorial is the statue of Eros in Piccadilly Circus.

He was born on 31 August, 1869, at the family home near Wimborne St. Giles, the son of the eighth Earl who had married the daughter of the third Marquess of Donegal through whom he inherited considerable interests in Northern Ireland. He was educated at Eton and Sandhurst, and in 1890 was given a commission in the 10th. Hussars cavalry regiment. In 1899 he married Lady Constance Grosvenor, the daughter of Earl Grosvenor, and grand-daughter of the first Duke of Westminster. From 1895-8 he was military secretary to Earl Brassey, the governor of Victoria in Australia. His Northern Ireland connections through his mother were very strong; from 1902 to 1912 he was the commanding officer of the Ninth Irish Horse regiment and at the same time, Lord Lieutenant of Belfast from 1904 to 1911, and Lord Mayor of Belfast in 1907. He later presented his Irish family seat, Belfast Castle, with 200 acres, to the city of Belfast in 1934. He was also Chancellor of Queen's University, Belfast, who awarded him an Honorary LL.D., and His Majesty's Lieutenant of the city of Antrim from 1911 to 1916. From 1901 to 1910 he was Lord Chamberlain to the Princess of Wales and continued to serve her when she became Queen until 1922, and then until 1936 he was Lord Steward of her majesty's household. During the First World war, he served as the Brigadier-General commanding the 1st. South West Mounted Brigade and of the 3rd. Cyclist Brigade.

His Dorset roots meant a great deal to him, and he served the county as its Lord Lieutenant from 1916 to 1952 and was the Chairman of the Dorset County Council from 1924 to 1946. He was also Provisional Grand Master of the Dorset Lodge of Freemasons from 1902 to 1952. In 1928 he provided a considerable financial grant for the establishment of Bryanston School at Blandford and served it as the first Chairman of the Governors. Among his wide other interests he was President of the English Church Union and a member of the National Church Assembly. He was Chairman of the National Advisory Council to the Ministry of Labour for Juvenile Employment for England and Wales, and Chairman of the Commission of the Development Fund Act from 1946 to 1948. He possessed a fine tenor voice, and had turned down the offer of a large sum of money by an American impresario to go on a concert tour of the United States. He was a vice president of the Royal Choral Society. He was a member of the Jockey Club and the Royal Yacht Squadron and a Younger Brother of Trinity House. As a very highly regarded public servant he received many honours and awards; he was made K.C.V.O. in 1906 and then G.C.V.O. in 1924. He was awarded the C.B.E. in 1919 and became a Privy Councillor in 1922. He was also a Bailiff Grand Cross of the Order of St. John of Jerusalem and a Grand Officer of the Legion of Honour. He died aged 91 on 25 March, 1961, and was buried in the parish church at Wimborne St. Giles, near the family estate. He was a very popular President of this Society and often sang solos at the Society's social events and annual dinners.

Shaiba Day

THE National War Memorial, the Cenotaph, was designed by the famous architect Sir Edwin Lutyens and unveiled by the King George V with a huge parade and solemn ceremony in Whitehall on Remembrance Day, November 11th. 1920. The President of the Society of Dorset Men, Lord Shaftesbury, who was also the Lord-Lieutenant of the County, together with the Secretary, William Watkins, and other representatives of the county and the Dorset Regiment – including three Chelsea Pensioners - came to the Cenotaph on 14 April 1921, to mark the anniversary of the battle of Shaiba in 1915, by laying a wreath in memory of the officers and men of the 2nd. Battalion who had died in the war. This was at the request of the Commanding Officer of the Battalion which was then stationed in Bangalore in India. This battle was part of the Mesopotamian campaign against the

Turks in which the Dorsets were part of a brigade involved in attacking a two-mile wide line of trenches on the slope of a hill with further lines 800 yards behind on the flat plain above. The Turks numbered about 20,000 men with thirty guns under the command of German officers. During the battle, the Dorset's commanding officer, Lieutenant-Colonel Rosher, was killed, but it resulted in an important victory for the British

Shaiba Day, April 14th. Lord Shaftesbury, as President of our Society, at the request of the 2nd Dorsets, lays their laurel wreath at the foot of the Cenotaph. Right, Mr. Watkins and Colour-Sergeant James.   Left, Mr. Stanley Galpin.

[Topical Press]

which relieved the city of Basra and enabled them to advance further up the Tigris to Amara. Most of the German officers had been killed and seven Dorset soldiers were awarded Distinguished Conduct Medals for bravery during the campaign. The ceremony at the Cenotaph was followed by a service in St. John's Church, Waterloo Road, at which Lord Shaftesbury sang "Be thou

Roll call of the 2nd Batallion of the Dorset Regiment at Basra, Mesopotamia

faithful unto death" from Mendelssohn's oratorio "St. Paul." The prayers included a Collect for the Society of Dorset Men which had been written by Bishop Wordsworth of Salisbury, for a service which had been held for the Society in St. Paul's Cathedral in February 1908. (1922 Y.B. p.43. account of battle in 1916-7 Y.Bk. p.119f).

The Year Book, copies of which were which sent to the Regiment, continued to contribute to this association by regularly printing articles about the deployment and recent activities of the Regiment as it had during the war. The 1923 issue contained a substantial article giving accounts of the various units who then had been serving in India, Ireland and Egypt. After considerable re-organisation various companies of the Territorials were dispersed in different towns in Dorset, with the Regimental Headquarters at Blandford and Squadron Headquarters at Dorchester, Sherborne and Blandford, with the Battalion Headquarters in Dorchester. The unnamed writer of this report ended it by saying, 'It would not be fitting to conclude without an acknowledgement of the interest always shown by the Society of Dorset Men in London in the welfare of the Territorials with whom it is connected. Before the war the Society provided a handsome challenge trophy for rifle competition, and during the war Dorset Units serving overseas had no kinder friends at home than its Members. The tangible expressions of their sympathy were much appreciated by all ranks on the fighting fronts. Material assistance is not now asked for, but a continuation of the personal interest shown by the Society in the past will materially help

our County Units to prepare themselves again honourably to fill their place in the scheme of national defence, should the time of trial come.'

During the peace-time years between the wars, the regiment continued to give the Year Book reports of its activities. Lt. Col. A.L. Ransome, the commander of the 1st. Battalion, wrote in 1930, 'to resume the doings of the Battalion during the past year.' Saying, 'the Society of Men in London have ever been our very good friends,' he describes the regiment's life in India following its move from Malta to Meerut in 1926. The commander of the 2nd. Battalion, also wrote 'to record the most important events for the period January 1926 to May 1930.' From 1927 they were stationed in Germany as part of the Army of Occupation on the Rhine. They 'found the Germans courteous, willing and obliging... the battalion was held in the highest esteem by the German community, who in return earned the respect of the battalion as a whole.' The occupation was finally ended in September, 1929, and the battalion returned to England and a civic reception at the Verne barracks on Portland. At the end of his report, the writer thanks the Society for laying a wreath on their behalf at the Cenotaph on the anniversary of Shaiba Day saying 'We would like to record our appreciation of this act of kindness.' The 1931 Year Book contained another long report from the 1st. Battalion, and also from the Dorset Heavy Brigade, who had won the Prince of Wales Cup at Sandown in a competition held by the National Artillery Association. The cup was presented to them at the Guildhall by the Lord Mayor of London in a ceremony which was attended by Members of the Society of Dorset Men, who then entertained the gunners to lunch at the Holborn Restaurant.

Then, in November 1930, the band of the 2nd. Battalion gave a concert to the Society of Dorset Men in the King George's Hall.

These relaxed events were brought to an end by the declaration of war with Germany once again in September, 1939. At the Annual General Meeting in October, the Society decided unanimously to re-introduce the Comforts Fund which had been so much appreciated during the previous war. As the war proceeded, the committee asked Members of the Society and readers of the Year Book to let them know the names of prisoners of war 'who are either Members of the Society of Dorset Men or from the County... When Mr. Bellamy, the treasurer, receives the names, tobacco or cigarettes will be forwarded to each man from the Comforts Fund . . . A line of remembrance and the solace of a pipe or cigarettes will let our County brethren know that they...are not forgotten by those in the Homeland.' There was a considerable response to this request, and many letters of thanks were received from prisoners of war as the war went on, grateful for the gifts, and for the interest shown in their welfare, particularly from some who had been among the first to be captured and had spent long years in captivity.

As the war ended, the commanding officer of the 2nd. Battalion, Lieut.-Col. O.G.W. White wrote to say what had happened to the Battalion after it was flown out of Burma in 1945. They were

---

THE DORSET YEAR BOOK 17

Special Notice — Prisoners-of-War

There may be known to Members of the Society and other readers of the *Dorset Year Book*, the names of prisoners-of-war who are either Members of the Society of Dorset Men or from the County.

The Officers and Committee are very anxious to get into touch with all the above-mentioned men and the Hon. Treasurer has asked me to draw special attention to this matter. It will therefore be greatly appreciated if full particulars relating to prisoners of war can be sent to:—

W. H. BELLAMY, Esq.,

Hon. Treasurer, The Society of Dorset Men,
Walter House, 418-22 Strand, London, W.C.2.

When Mr. Bellamy receives the names, tobacco or cigarettes will be forwarded to each man from the Comforts Fund, which was created at the outbreak of war for this purpose.

Let each and all of us do our very best to relieve the monotony of internment. A line of remembrance and the solace of a pipe or cigarettes will let our County brethren know that they are by no means forgotten by those in the Homeland.

On behalf of the Officers and Committee please accept our most grateful thanks for your active co-operation in this good cause.

Ashley C. Rogers.

Hon. Editor.

THE DORSET YEAR BOOK 135

Prisoners of War

Mr. W. H. Bellamy, the Hon. Treasurer, has received many post cards from Prisoners of War, and extracts from six of the cards recently received are shown below :—

Kriegsgefangenenlager   Datum 24th September, 1943.

Dear Sir—I wish to thank you and all members of the Society of Dorset Men for parcel of cigarettes received. I can assure you they were very acceptable.   Yours faithfully—F. RIDOUT, 13677

Kriegsgefangenenlager.   Datum 5th October, 1943.

Dear Sir—Thank you very much for your letter of the 12th Sept., it is very kind of the Society to remember me to the extent of sending cigarettes, and I very much appreciate it. This is a large camp here, but the Red Cross gives us plenty of attention and consequently we are all very fit and happy. I am hoping to participate in some of the Society's activities on my return home, which I hope will not be too distant.
          Yours sincerely—(Sgt.) HARRY LANGFORD 5512

Kriegsgefangenenlager.   Datum 10th October, 1943

Dear Sir—Thank you very much for your letter of September, 43. I have received a parcel of two hundred cigarettes, I believe they are from the Society. Cigarettes to us mean such a great help. I am a Dorset man, born and bred, and to me it is still the finest little place in the world. Thanking you once again.   Yours sincerely—G. W. HARRIS, 6848

Kriegsgefangenenlager.   Datum 10th October, 1943

Dear Sir—In answer to you letter dated September, 1943, I have received two parcels of cigarettes for which I owe you and your Society many thanks. Wishing you all a very merry Christmas and tons of luck for 1944.   I remain, Yours Sincerely—L/Cpl. T. H. LEGG, 1125

Kriegsgefangenenlager.   Datum 12th October, 1943

Dear Sir—I am in receipt of your letter 19/9/43, and thank you very much for the kind interest you shew in myself and fellow country-men in this unfortunate state of captivity. This is my third year and it could be much worse. I have never met anyone from Dorset, but many soldiers who passed through our fine County, and who treasure happy memories of it. I am, Sir, Yours faithfully—(Sgt.) D. W. HARRINGTON, 11970

Kriegsgefangenenlager.   Datum 17th October, 1943

Dear Sir—In reply to your letter of the 13th September, 1943, I would like to convey my grateful thanks for your kindness in despatching cigarettes to me, will inform you of the arrival of them. Wishing you all the very best of luck.
          I am, Sir, Yours faithfully—Leading Seaman Wm. LEANEY, R.N., 18588.

All the above-mentioned men are Prisoners of War in various camps at M. Stammlager and we all hope that this will be their last Christmas in captivity.
          Editor.

'fortunate to be selected as the Battalion to represent the English Infantry...to take part in the occupation of Japan.' After re-forming in India, they arrived in Japan in April 1946, where they were detailed to be the first British Battalion to undertake public duties in Tokyo, which involved sharing the Guard on the Imperial Palace with the 1st. Cavalry Division of the United States Army.

There they 'performed what is...the greatest of all Infantry Ceremonies', trooping the Regimental Colour on the Plaza of the Imperial Palace. White says, 'For those twenty of us who had crossed the River Brahmaputra in 1944 it was the end of a very long march and

we know how much our old comrades would have given to have been with us in Tokyo on the morning of June 28th.'

White says that there were several high-ranking officers at the parade, both English and American, and, together with himself, 'Among the Kohima

THE INSCRIPTION ON THE MEMORIAL AT KOHIMA.
In memory of all ranks of the 2nd. Batallion of The Dorset Regiment who fell in action in these hills between April to June 1944
WHO'S AFEAR'D?

veterans on parade was Brigadier R.S. McNaught, DSO who commanded us at Kohima..' After describing their base on the south coast of Shiloku Island, the mountains of which he says 'recall the exhausting climbs we had to make in the Naga Hills in Assam two years ago', he ends his report, 'before closing this brief account...I want to take this opportunity of thanking once again all those grand people of Dorset who so readily answered my various appeals for cigarettes and comforts not only during the exhausting days in Burma last year but even to this day, continue to work on our behalf. I would say that now is quite as important as then – we are 12,000 miles away from home...further away than any Dorset soldiers have ever been before…On my return to the U.K. I hope to be able to thank a number of you personally for all you have done during the last three years – and to all of you we send our greetings from Japan.' (Photos of parade on ps. 27/8 1946/7 Y.B.)

During the years following the war, the Year Book continued to receive reports from the regiment as it changed and adapted to new situations and challenges. After serving in the Army of Occupation on the Rhine, the 1st Battalion was sent to Austria in 1948, where they carried out garrison duties guarding the British and Allied Headquarters in Vienna, which was in the Russian occupation zone, although the central section of the city was the international sector, under the four-power administration. They were housed in barracks built for Hitler's S.S., 'So there is running hot water…central heating, nice large airy rooms…palatial messes for the officers and sergeants'. The Society sent some music to the Regiment and received an appreciative letter back from the Band President; 'I thank you very much indeed for your letter, forwarding copies of "Praise 'o Dorset," "The Prickety Bush" and the "Turmit Hoer." 'We thank you for your expression of good wishes to the Regiment.' The commanding officer,

Lt. Col. L.J. Wood, wrote to the Editor of the Year Book; 'Perhaps you might think it worth saying in the Year Book that if any Dorset folk are holidaying in Austria…I should be delighted if they got in touch with me so that… arrangements could be made for them to visit us.' After two years in Austria the Battalion was moved to Hong Kong, and then from1954 to 1955, they were sent to Korea, just a year after the end of the fighting there. A photo of the Regimental Band playing at the quayside of Kowloon, as the Battalion departed, moved the Editor of the Year Book, (C. H. Dennett) to write, 'what a host of nostalgic memories this photo conjures up to those members who cherish recollections of…when the Regimental Band always played selections at the Society's Annual Dinner – a practice revived in October at the Dinner at Dorchester Corn Exchange in welcome to the 1st. Battalion on its return.'

The Band (Bandmaster J. Plant) plays the Batallion off for Korea from the quayside at Kowloon, Hong Kong on 11 August 1954.

Describing their winter in Korea, their commander, Lieut. Col. White, described training under sub-zero conditions, and said how much they had appreciated the arrival in February of the winter comforts which had been collected as a result of the Colonel-of-the-Regiment appeal; 'We are all most grateful to our good friends and well wishers at home, especially to those members of the Society who sent their gifts to us last winter...should these lines reach them we hope they will appreciate how much we value their generosity.' At the end of his long and informative article, he writes 'One final word...to say how much we of the Dorset Regiment appreciate that excellent publication, The Dorset Year Book. Its arrival is not only eagerly anticipated but it is thoroughly read and passed around the Battalion until it becomes a tattered pamphlet. We offer our sincere congratulations to Mr. Dennett on his publication.'

On 21st. May, 1958, the county regiments of Dorset and Devon were amalgamated to form the Devonshire and Dorset Regiment. This took place at a ceremonial parade in pouring rain in Minden in Germany. The Colonel of the new regiment was Major General G. N. Wood, who for the previous six years had been Colonel of the Dorset Regiment. Although this was recognised as sacrificing something of the individual character of each Regiment and its connections with its own history, the Territorial battalions, though forming part of the new regiment, retained their identity unchanged. The 4th. Dorsets kept their old badge and continued to occupy the Dorchester barracks, and the Regimental Museum remained at the Keep. The Regimental Depot in the Dorchester barracks was closed down and the main Regimental Headquarters was moved to Exeter, though a 'token 'Regimental Headquarters' with a small, mainly civilian staff, was retained as an outpost of the main Headquarters at Exeter. The association with the Society was continued chiefly through those serving or who had served in the Regiment who were Members of the Society, and especially through the Year Book, which provided the main means of communication and information as it continued to include articles received from the Regiment in its pages. But inevitably, the close bonds forged between the Society and the Regiment through the two world wars by the Comfort Fund and the number of the Society's Members serving with the Regiment, loosened as memories faded and the new Regiment lost its exclusive Dorset identity and its direct descent from its history.

For very many years the continuing connection between the Society and the regiment was kept alive by the personal involvement in both of one man, Brigadier A.E.C. Bredin. He had been commissioned in the Dorsetshire Regiment in 1931, had served with it during the war, and had been the second in command of the Battalion when it took part in the Normandy landings on D-Day, 6th. June, 1944. Subsequently, after promotion to Brigadier, he was Colonel of the Devonshire and Dorset Regiment from 1967 to 1977, and was President of the Dorset Regiment Association from 1962 until 1988. Although the commanding officers of the Regiment were always accepted as Honorary Members of the Society, he

Brigadier Bredin

was already a personal Member from 1948. At the Regiment Association's annual service at the Cenotaph in Whitehall, in 1949 he laid a wreath on behalf of the Society, and continued to lay a wreath there for very many years afterwards.

But change came again, and the 1966/7 Year Book contained an article announcing that the Government intended to reorganise the T.A. "which in effect meant the disappearance of the Dorset Regiment in its present form" at the end of March 1967. In 1972 the designation changed again as it ceased to be 'The Wessex Volunteers' and became 'C. Company, (Dorsets) 1st. Battalion, the Wessex Regiment.' These were not peaceful times for the Regiment, as, after service in Malta, the Battalion was moved to Northern Ireland, where only three days after they arrived, eighteen year old Private Philip Steinford from North Devon was

killed by a land mine detonated from over the border in Eire. Two more soldiers were killed when their vehicle on patrol was ambushed and destroyed by two hundred pounds of explosives hidden under the road.

The Regiment continued to serve periods in Ireland up to and after the end of the Troubles, as changes in its structure and designation continued to be made. In April, 1995, the 1st. Battalion was deployed to Bosnia for a sixth month tour of duty as part of the United Nations engagement there. At the Society's County Dinner in October, the President and Members sent their greetings to 'Our County regiment carrying out their hazardous duties in Bosnia.' Among the guests was the Colonel of the Regiment, General Sir John Wilsey, who proposed a toast to the Regiment. A reply was received from the 1st. Battalion, expressing their appreciation of the message, which ends with "Semper Fidelis"-'Who's a-fear'd?'

In the following Year Book he reports on the formation of the Rifles and where they were then serving, some – including the Territorials - in Afghanistan, and others in Germany and Gibralter. He ends by saying that 'The Rifles have every intention of maintaining the close links with Dorset which the Devon and Dorsets nurtured over the years...It is early days for the Rifles, but they are determined that the people of Dorset will be able to feel very proud of the achievements of their new County Regiment.' During a year in what Col. Nicholls describes as 'undoubtedly...the toughest in the Regiment's history' the Rifles were heavily engaged in Afghanistan, which cost the lives of 34 officers and soldiers killed in action and many seriously wounded. But he was also pleased to be able to say that 'a great deal has been achieved in terms of maintaining contact with our places of origin – our counties, cities and towns.' 'The towns of Dorset have shown tremendous support throughout the year.' Among the towns in which they paraded and were granted Freedom were Shaftesbury, Poole and Wimborne. In Dorchester a Service of Remembrance was held in St. Peter's Church in which six of those lost in Afghanistan were remembered, and a 'hugely well-supported' Homecoming Parade was made through the town.

The following year, more Freedoms were received from Bournemouth, Bridport and Blandford.

Col. Nicholls' reports show that the long history of the association of this Society with the Regiment, through all its changes, and through the world wars of the last century and the continuing wars in this, in which those serving have fought and died, continues to be appreciated and maintained, especially through the Year Books, which keep the Members of the Society informed and up-to-date with the Regiment's activities.

The Keep Military Museum, Dorchester, formerly the Regimental Depot

The Society Between the Wars

FOLLOWING the ending of the War, the Society returned to its peacetime programme and looked forward to celebrating its 21st. Anniversary in 1925. But then it was shaken by the deaths close together of four of its best-known and leading figures. The Society's first President, Sir Frederick Treves, died suddenly at Lausanne in France on 7 December, 1923. Treves had been a very active and enthusiastic President, contributing many articles on Dorset history to the Year Book, and his death was felt keenly by the members. His funeral took place at St. Peter's Church in Dorchester on 2 January 1924. Among those who packed the crowded church were Lord Dawson of Penn, there to represent King George V, and Lord Howe, representing Queen Alexandra. In 1902 Treves had operated on her husband King Edward VII and saved his life. Treves' wife was represented by another leading member of the Society and former Editor of the Year Book, Newman Flower. At the request of Lady Treves the funeral was organised by WilliamWatkins, the Society's Secretary, and the hymns and psalms for the service were chosen by Thomas Hardy who had succeeded Treves as President, and included a hymn which had been sung at the funeral service of Hardy's father at Stinsford in 1892. Hardy also wrote a poem in tribute, which was published in The Times and included in the 1924 Year Book; a verse of which has been engraved on Treves's grave in the Weymouth Avenue cemetery. Among the wreaths placed on the grave was one from the King and a cross from Queen Alexandria. Treves' coffin was draped with the Society's flag, and the Society's wreath bore a card with a verse from Treves' old schoolmaster, William Barnes.

An even greater shock to the Society was the very sudden and unexpected death of the Society's greatly loved and respected Secretary, William Watkins. The 1925 Year Book begins with a letter dated March 1925, from Thomas Hardy to William Watkins, in response to Watkins decision to retire from office that year. Hardy says:

"It is difficult to realise the Society of Dorset Men in London without yourself as the warm-hearted & enthusiastic Honorary Secretary. All these years – twenty-one I believe – you have been its mainstay, never sparing yourself for the good of every Dorset man who has needed your help. But we are glad to know that your friendly eye will still be upon the Society, & are sure that you will not be forgotten by Dorset Men in London, & Dorset Men in Dorset, & indeed, Dorset Men all over the world. "

Yours most sincerely
Thomas Hardy

The first article in the Year Book is one by Watkins himself, giving an account of what he refers to as his "Stewardship" of the Society. Tracing his story of the Society from his first arriving in London in 1895 and having it pointed out to him that Dorset was almost the only county in England not to have a Society in London. After the successful launch of the Society in 1904, he describes travelling abroad and meeting Dorset men in South Africa, Australia and New Zealand, which led to the establishment of associated Societies overseas. When the War broke out in 1914, many County Societies suspended their operations but Dorset determined to carry on. Watkins arranged for hospital visitation to the wounded and for creature comforts to be sent to all the fighting men of Dorset in the various theatres of war – which even included a brass band for the Dorset Regiment in France. Celebrating the successful growth of the Society he said "We are now approaching the time when we shall have one thousand Home Members…and I shall feel very proud indeed when it is announced at the Dinner on Dorset Day, the Vust Monday in May, that this number has been reached."

William Watkins, was active in much of the life of the county as well as the Society. He was a magistrate and also a member of the Dorset Field Club, the County Museum and the Dorchester Debating Society. He was fond of athletics and played cricket for the Dorchester Cricket Club, and when the Dorset County Football Association was formed he became its Honorary Secretary and continued in that office for several years, until he left Dorchester to go to London, when he handed over this position to Mark C. Frowde. In July, 1922, William Watkins presented Frowde, who had become the President of the Dorset County Football Association, with a Cup 'in recognition of his services to the association for over a quarter of a century.' The cup was one of two originally commissioned by the Football Association to replace the F.A. cup which had been stolen. The other cup was used to replace the stolen cup and this one was placed in the vaults until the Dorset F. A. took ownership of it. Frowde donated the Cup back to the Association 'to be a perpetual trophy' with a cheque for £100 to buy medals for a competition among the schoolboys of Dorset.

Mr. M. C. Frowde J.P.

WINNERS: Weymouth Central Boys' School, 1935. Teacher Bill Stuckey is standing behind the pupils on the right hand side

Now known as the Mark Frowde Cup, it is still being played for by school teams today

On 19 April, 1925, Watkins spent the day with Thomas Hardy and his wife at Max Gate. Hardy's small dog Wessex, which had a fierce reputation against all strangers, but knew Watkins well, and accepted him as a friend, is reported to have acted very strangely towards him on this occasion and appeared to be very troubled by his presence. At the end of the day Watkins returned to the King's Arms in Dorchester where he was staying. Later that night he died of a heart attack. Long obituaries appeared in the County Chronicle. His funeral was held in the Congregational Church in South Street where he was a member, and the building was crowded with friends and representatives of all the businesses and organisations he had been connected with, including the Dorset Regiment and many members of the Society and of the Hardy Players. The flag of the Society which had been used to drape the coffin of Sir Frederick Treves the year before, was used again to cover the coffin of the Society's Secretary. Thomas Hardy and his wife attended the burial in the Weymouth Avenue cemetery, very close to that of Treves. Among the tributes placed on the grave was one from the Hardy Players which bore a quotation from Hardy's The Woodlanders; "He was a good man, and did good things." And one "From the Kut Survivors" in acknowledgement of Watkins' and the Society's efforts to relieve the suffering of those who had been imprisoned by the Turks after the terrible siege and fall of Kut in Mesopotamia during the War in April, 1916.

Sir Frederick Treves

It is the custom now of the present members of the Society to carry the flag of the Society each year on 19th April, to the Weymouth Avenue cemetery and to place floral tributes on the adjacent graves of their first President and first Secretary.

**Society Members at the graves
of the Society's Founders**
Left to Right: Rev Dr John Travell, Hayne Russell,
Trevor Vacher-Dean, Peter Lush, David Forrester,
Paul Snow, Jill Vacher-Dean, Bev Lenthall,
Chris Carter and Andy Hutchings.
Photo by Michel Hooper-Immins.

A month before William Watkins death, in March, 1925, the death had been announced of the Society's fifth President, Sir Stephen Collins. Born in Swanage in 1847, Collins had left to make his fortune in London when he was 14. He had followed his father in working in the Purbeck stone quarrying industry, and succeeded in establishing himself in business in London importing Purbeck stone for the many new important London buildings then being erected as London vastly expanded during the latter half of the 19th. century. He was actively engaged in local government and public service, becoming a County Councillor and then Member of Parliament for Kennington, and received a knighthood in 1913, the year he became President of this Society. He retained his strong association with his home county, and particularly the Congregational church in Swanage which he had attended as a child. He had given generously to the fund for building a new church and manse, and had served as President of the Dorset Association of Congregational Churches.

Then, less than two weeks after William Watkins, came the death of Harry Pouncy, on 28th. April 1925. This was less unexpected since Pouncy had been seriously ill for more than a year, but his loss was a cause for much sadness both to the Society and throughout the County where he was particularly well-known. Pouncy was a personal friend of Thomas Hardy, who valued his knowledge of the County and its life and customs. Pouncy had been a journalist, working for the County Chronicle, and then he became Secretary of the Dorset Farmers' Union which made him known as a friend to every farmer in the County. But Pouncy's particular fame was as a lecturer, both throughout Dorset and to the Society in London. According to his obituary in the Society's Year Book, "there was no one who could describe the Wessex of history and romance so delightfully as he…his knowledge of the rural folk and their habits was such that he could impersonate them to the life. Given a lantern picture of a Dorset yokel, Mr. Pouncy could make the character live." "He was widely known for his lectures on "Old Dorset Rustic Wit and Humour"…and no man was more capable to lecture on Dorset, its dialect, manners, folklore, archaeology, literature and humour." When 250 members of the Society in London made a special visit to Dorchester in June 1906, at the invitation of the Mayor, Harry Pouncy acted as their tour guide, and his annual lectures to the Society in London were a very popular part of the Society's yearly programme. His most outstanding contribution to the Society, and his most lasting legacy,

were his contributions to the Year Books during the long years of War. Pouncy fully documented in the most extraordinary detail, the involvement of the different battalions of the Dorset Regiment in every sphere of the War, from the trenches in France, to Gallipoli, India, Mesopotamia and Palestine, including the accounts of the experiences of individuals in every branch of the services, which now provide invaluable information for anyone wishing to know more about the events and experiences of that War, and especially are an outstanding resource for anyone seeking genealogical information about their family history during that period of time.

H. Llewellyn Watkins

H. Llewelyn Watkins was the eldest son of William Watkins, and took over from his father as the Society's second Secretary. He was born in 1887, and when he was seventeen he was present with his father at the meeting in his father's office in July 1904, when the decision was made to form the Society. He served as a captain in the army during the First World War, and then took up a government appointment in Canada. He returned to London in time for the Society's 21st anniversary in 1925, when his father announced his intention to retire, and told Llewelyn, who was acting as his Assistant Secretary, that he wished him to succeed him. After William Watkin's sudden death in April that year, the Society immediately appointed Llewelyn as their next Secretary, a post he held for twelve years, until 1937. Like his father, he was held in considerable affection and regard, and his commitment to the Society was recognised and appreciated. When the Editor of the Year Book, Stanley Galpin retired in 1932, leaving a gap in the publication for two years because another Editor could not be found, Llewelyn took on this responsibility as well, and produced the next two issues for1935 and1936, when Ashley Rogers accepted the Editorship. After he retired as Secretary in 1937, he was made an Honorary Life Member. He died, aged sixty-five, at his home in Somerset on 16 February, 1952.

The Society's memorial to William Watkins

THE Society had intended to make a presentation to its Honorary Secretary at its 21st. Anniversary Dinner on Dorset Day in May 1925, in tribute to his unequalled service to the Society as its founder and organiser for twenty- one years. His sudden and unexpected death in April left them with the dilemma of deciding what to do with the money that had been warmly and generously donated. William Watkins' son, Llewellyn, had been elected the new Secretary in his father's place. Wondering what to do with the money, he discovered that the Dorset County Hospital in Trinity Street needed an Ophthalmic Ward, but had not been able to provide one because of the expense. The Society therefore decided to hand the money to the Hospital to help provide the new unit. As the amount was not enough to cover the whole expense necessary, the Watkins family themselves provided the rest of the money needed.

At a special ceremony on 17 February, 1927, the members of the Society from London and the county gathered for the official opening of the new Department, as a memorial to their much missed Honorary Secretary. In presenting the gift on behalf of the Society to Lord Ellenborough, the Chairman of the Hospital committee, Llewellyn Watkins said, "I think you will agree with me that no more fitting memorial could be made for him than this Ophthalmic Ward...represented in that room are the loving thoughts of hundreds of Dorset people...at home and abroad. And what we are giving you today is symbolical, in that it is part of the very soul of our Society." He then handed Lord Ellenborough a brass dedication plate, mounted on oak, with the inscription:

> The Ophthalmic room was presented by the Society of Dorset Men in London to the Dorset County Hospital in affectionate remembrance of William Watkins J.P., Honorary Secretary of the Society from its formation, 7th. July 1904, to 19th April 1925.

In replying, Lord Ellenborough, thanking the Society for the presentation, said that the tablet would be placed in a conspicuous position in the Hospital.

The Annual General Meeting in 1928, began with a tribute to the Society's second President, Thomas Hardy, who had died in January that year, and reported on the deaths of several older members. Even so, the membership had increased by 18 to 1,083 home members and there were also 605 overseas members, giving a total of nearly 1,700. The Deputy Treasurer, George Hatcher, was also able to report an improvement in the financial position of the Society, and increased payments had been able to be made from the Benevolent Fund. Mr. Dugdale remarked that it was gratifying that for the first time in the history of the Society they were out of debt. The report on the 1929 AGM in the 1930 Year Book begins with the statement 'Robust well-being was evident in the large attendance of members of the Society at the 26th Annual Meeting.' The Society was still being led by those who had been the original members in 1904, but these were getting older and becoming fewer. J. C. Swinburne-Hanham, was still the Chairman, having been first elected in 1904. In contrast with the previous year, he had to report that 'the Society had sustained a loss of many of its members' and the membership was now 1,070 home members and 587 overseas. The Secretary, H. Llewellyn Watkins, reporting on the Year Book, proposed a hearty vote of appreciation and thanks to the Editor, Stanley Galpin, for his 'gift of a tremendous weight of paper for it for over twenty years - its size and the printing of 3,000 copies showed what a wonderful help these annual gifts had been.'

Swinburne-Hanham began the 1930 AGM by congratulating the Society on having reached the 25th. Yearly Meeting, and said 'it was a great thing for the Society not only to have been in existence but to have been flourishing for over a quarter of a century.' In spite of the deaths of 'many esteemed and valued members' the numbers of home members had slightly increased. The proposal that the Society should 'henceforward be known as the Society of Dorset Men' was unanimously acclaimed, and 'in conformity with a wish expressed in the County, become an institution without... differentiations between members living in the County and members in town.' The change of name was officially adopted at a special meeting on 28 April, 1931.

The AGM in November, 1931 again had to report 'the passing of many of its old and valued members as shown in the long obituary list in the 1931 Year Book.' Among them were two of the oldest members of the committee Charles Rogers ('Wold Char'l) and J.R. Tomkins. The national economic situation was also affecting the membership of the Society, with some members having felt the need to resign their membership. The subsequent loss of income meant that the Society had to report a deficit in its accounts of £27 and had to take money from the Benevolent Fund in order to balance the books. The larger Year Book had cost nearly £50 more to produce, although the Deputy Treasurer assured the meeting that 'it was singularly good value, literary, moral and avoirdupois.' The Editor of the Year Book, Stanley Galpin, announced in an Editorial letter to his readers in the 1932 edition, headed 'Hail And Farewell!' that this was to be the last one he would produce. This took the members by surprise and caused considerable concern. Galpin was only the second editor that the publication had had, having taken over from its first Editor, the distinguished journalist Newman Flower, who had given up in 1920 owing to a break down in his health. The difficulty in finding another Editor meant that the Society was unable to publish the Year Book again until 1935, when the Society's Secretary, H.Ll. Watkins, took over and managed to produce the book again in 1935 and 1936, when Ashley Rogers accepted the responsibility and continued as Editor during the War years until1950.

Without the Year Book, there is no record of the Society's meetings between 1932 and 1935, when the members came together again in March 1935 for their AGM. At the opening of the meeting the members stood in silence to remember their Chairman, J. C. Swinburne-Hanham, who had died in January that year. He had been the Society's Chairman since its beginning in 1904. The Secretary, who was the son of the founder Secretary, William Watkins, told the meeting that he was now the only one left who saw Mr. Swinburne-Hanham elected as Chairman at the meeting which decided to form the Society. The Society had continued to lose members by death and resignation. The meeting heard that there were now 899 home members and 539 overseas.

H. Ll. Watkins, having served the Society as its Secretary for 22 years, resigned in 1937 and was succeeded by Harry Dunn from Bridport, who had been a member of the Society for 25 years. The following year, Dunn reported that the Society had been through a difficult year, but had emerged well. They had become affiliated to the English Counties Societies Conference which enabled members to enter competitions for various sports and games. W. H. Bellamy, who was now the Treasurer, was able to report that the accounts were in a very good position and said that 'the members themselves did it. If only they paid their subscriptions in the future as they had during the past year they would do well.'

The Society in the Second World War 1939-1945

THE Society's Annual General Meeting in October 1939 was held a month after the war had been declared. It was the last AGM until the end of the war in 1945. At the meeting it was reported that 'the Society was forging ahead'. The Golden Jubilee of the Dorset County Council had been celebrated, and the Year Book would contain a new educational feature to find the best student in a Dorset school. Then under Any Other Business it was decided that because of blackout regulations it would not be possible to hold any social functions. It was also unanimously agreed to create a Comforts Fund for those serving in Dorset units of the forces as the Society had provided during the First World War. In spite of paper shortages the Society managed to continue to produce its Year Book each year throughout the war. Copies of each throughout the war were received by the King and members of the royal family, and also the Prime Minister, Winston Churchill.

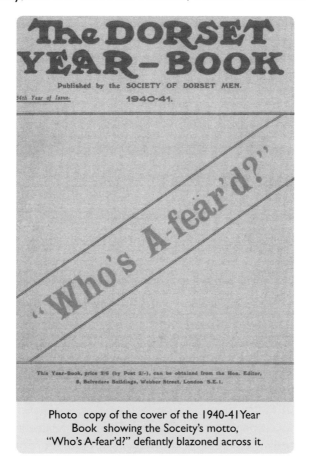

Photo copy of the cover of the 1940-41 Year Book showing the Soceity's motto, "Who's A-fear'd?" defiantly blazoned across it.

Winston Churchill

Churchill had been the guest of honour at the Society's Annual Dinner at the Holborn Restaurant on 'Dorset Day', May 6th. 1924.

Reporting the event, the Year Book said, "The Right Hon. Winston Churchill, P.C., arrived late – very late – with the Blue Vinny, and shared in the tremendous cheering which greeted the entry of Dorset's far-famed product...The President, (Captain the Rt. Hon. F. E. Guest) drew a warm cheer from the company when he referred to the presence of his distinguished cousin, Mr. Winston Churchill, who, at last, after waiting forty-eight years, was beginning to realise that he was a Dorset man."

In his address, Churchill commented on the "remarkable" fact that among those present there were men from several places overseas. He said. "When one saw a single county bringing in representatives from the four corners of the earth – from Rhodesia, New Zealand, India, and from every part of the British Empire... he was very proud indeed to have been permitted to come there, and he was very obliged to their Secretary for having impressed so strongly upon him, the fact that...he was a Dorset man."   The importance of history and the British Empire "upon which... the best of civilisation in the whole world depends" were his main themes, saying "Do not let us despise the past...it is only time that dignifies."   Complimenting the Society on joining themselves together "to cherish...that sense of love of county and of home" he went on to say that "Local patriotism was the only true foundation of national patriotism, and national patriotism was the only true foundation of good world's citizenship."

orty Years On   1924

THE Society of Dorset Men, who are celebrating their diamond jubilee this week, heard Sir Winston Churchill acknowledge some time ago that his family belonged to their county rather than Devon. Appropriately, for Harrow's greatest pupil, the occasion was the Society's annual dinner in London 40 years ago to-day.

Sir Winston agreed that he himself was really a Dorset man, even though his ancestor, the great Duke of Marlborough, came from Musbury in Devon.

Press cutting from the Society's Diamond Jubilee in 1964
recalling Churchill acknowledging his Dorset roots

"A VOICE ACROSS THE CENTURIES."

Spirit of Marlborough—"Greetings dear Prime Minister! Your ancestor bids you welcome to Dorset, the birthplace of our sires."

❊ ❊ ❊ ❊ ❊

John Churchill, the first Duke of Marlborough, was the son of Winston Churchill of Glanvilles Wootton and, to quote the encyclopædia, "of a good Dorset family."

———

Winston Spencer Churchill, the Prime Minister, is the grandson of the 7th Duke of Marlborough. During the year he visited Dorset, inspecting defence preparations and watching manœuvres.

A cartoon from the 1940 Year Book

Winston Churchill in 1924

Colonel Llewellin (1893-1957)

THE demands of the war on its members and officers seriously affected the running of the Society. In 1940, the AGM was abandoned because of air raids. It was not until after the war had ended that the Society was able to hold another AGM. and to resume its Annual Dinner. In 1941 the Dorset Printing Works in London which produced the Year Book was destroyed in the bombing but it was able to be transferred to Weymouth where it continued to be printed throughout the war. Both the Secretary and the Assistant Secretary resigned and Ernest Gale was appointed. Then in 1941 he was also called up and another Secretary, Harry Harvey was then elected. The war made particularly heavy demands on the Society's Chairman, Col. J. Llewellin, who was given considerable government responsibility in the running of the war. As the war began he was Civil Lord of the Admiralty. He was then appointed Parliamentary Secretary to the Ministry of Supply and then to the Ministry of Aircraft Production where he was the spokesman in the House of Commons for the Minister, Lord Beaverbrook. He then became Minister of War Transport and a member of the Cabinet as the President of the Board of Trade and then Minister for Aircraft Production. In 1942 he was sent to Washington as Minister Resident for supply when the Atlantic U-Boat war on the vital convoys was at its height. His last wartime appointment was as Minister for Food from 1943 to 1945.

JOHN Jestyn Llewellin was born in Chevening, Kent and educated at Eton and University College, Oxford. He served in the Dorset Royal Garrison Artillery in the First World War and was awarded the Military Cross in 1917. He became a member of the Bar in 1921 and Conservative member of Parliament for Uxbridge in 1929. His first government appointment was as Parliamentary Secretary to the Post Master General in 1931. He then became the Parliamentary Secretary to First Commissioner of Works, and an Assistant Government whip, before becoming civil lord to the Admiralty in 1937. After his war service he was created a Baron in 1945 and a Deputy Lieutenant for Dorset. He was Chairman of the Dorset Quarter Sessions, President of the Royal Society for the Prevention of Accidents, President of the Chambers of Commerce of the British Empire, and a member of the BBC. General Advisory Council. In 1953 he became the first Governor General of the Federation of Rhodesia and Nyasaland. He was appointed a CBE. In 1939, and then GBE. in 1953. He was President of the Society of Dorset Men from 1944 until his death in 1957, in Government House in Salisbury, Rhodesia.

THE CHAIRMAN

COLONEL THE RIGHT HON. J. J. LLEWELLIN, C.B.E., M.C., T.D., M.P.

The Society in the Post-War Years

New Officers of the Society

At the last Annual General Meeting, Mr. F. C. H. Dennett was appointed Hon. Secretary and Major C. B. G. Grassby, Hon. Treasurer of the Society. Both of these gentlemen were educated at the Dorchester Grammar School and have achieved success in their respective professions. Many members and friends of the Society have not yet had the opportunity of seeing or meeting the new officers, and for this reason I am publishing their photographs, with a brief outline of their activities.

Mr. F. C. H. DENNETT,

Mr. F. C. H. Dennett
Hon. Secretary

Educated at Dorchester Grammar School ; enlisted Dorset Battery R.F.A. (T), proceeded to India ; Commissioned in Indian Army ; served N.W. Frontier (Afghanistan Campaign and later) ; Qualified as member of the Association of Certified Accountants and Auditors and commenced in practice on own account in 1928 ; Founder Secretary, Sidcup and District Chamber of Commerce 1937 ; Secretary, Bexley Cottage Hospital ; 1941-1945 Organiser and Section Capt. Fire Guard Service ; Organiser and Secretary, Traders Mutual Aid Pact and Retail Distributors Transport Pool.

Major C. B. G. Grassby
Hon. Treasurer

Educated at Dorchester Grammar School ; 1914-18 War, served in the Royal Engineers and Royal Flying Corps with rank of Lieutenant in the latter ; In business as a Monumental Sculptor in Dorchester until 1925, in Blandford until 1933, and in Sidcup at the present time ; 1940-45 War, L.D.V. and H.G. ; Major and 2 i/c 57th Kent Bn. and later London A.A. (Rocket) Btry at Shooters Hill. Is a Member of Chislehurst and Sidcup Rotary Club, Old Contemptibles, British Legion, and President of H.G. Old Comrades Association.

A.C.R.

Major C. B. G. GRASSBY,

Photo of page from the 1946-47 year book reporting the appointment of Mr. F. C. H. Dennett as Secretary and Major C. B. G. Grassby as Treasurer. Under this new leadership the Society was able to recover from the effects of the war as it restored its activities and gained new members.

From the beginning, the main administrative and driving force of the Society has been its succession of Honorary Secretaries, some of whom gave many years of devoted service. Its founder Secretary, William Watkins, retired after 21 years to be followed by his son Llewellyn, who held the office for twelve years from 1925 to 1937.

From 1939, the national emergency and the demands of the Second World War disrupted the regular peacetime organisation of the Society, as members departed to serve in the forces and other wartime occupations. So there were three Secretaries from 1937 to 1942; S.H.J. Dunn, E.G.Gale and Harry Harvey. Then F.C H. Dennett was elected and was able to see the Society through to the end of the War in 1945, and together with a new treasurer, Major C.B.G.Grassby, now released from the army, they returned the Society to its pre-war firm footing. Dennett continued as Secretary until he died in March, 1961. From 1951 to 1960, he also took on the heavy role as Editor of the Year Book. He was followed as Secretary by W.T.G. Perrott, who had already been acting as Dennett's Assistant. Perrott was born in Bridport, and after War service in the Reconnaissance Corps, had been engaged as an interpreter in a camp for German prisoners of war. He continued as Secretary until 1969, when he was succeeded by J.C.R. Prewer who after ten years in the post was followed by Gordon Hine in 1979, who then became the Society's longest serving Secretary, finally retiring after 25 years in 2004, when our present very dedicated and highly regarded Secretary, Hayne Russell took over.

Gordon Hine

Described as 'A towering personality at the centre of the organisation,' Gordon Hine became a member of the Society in 1953 and a member of the committee in 1958. During the Second World War, as an officer in the Royal Corps of Signals, he saw service in India, Iraq and Syria and then in the Western Desert in Montgomery's successful campaign. Before he was demobbed he was in charge of communications for the Victory Parade in London, in June, 1946. As a qualified Chartered Quantity Surveyor, in 1954 he accepted a three year contract in Australia working on buildings for the 1956 Olympic Games. Returning to Dorset he was for three decades a popular county, district and town councillor. He was three times Mayor of Shaftesbury, and an Honorary Freeman of both Gillingham and Shaftesbury. With his father, he built up a collection of fairground musical instruments and organs with which they gave performances for charity, raising some £6,000 over forty years.

One of Gordon Hine's first innovations was to introduce a regular Newsletter for members. The first, consisting of two typewritten pages on A4, was sent out in September, 1979, and was well enough received for him to continue, with the next issue in March, 1980. This gave information about the Year Book, and reports on the annual Dinner, held at Portland Heights, the winner of the Hambro Golf Cup (A.W.Caddy) and gave details about the next London Dinner, due to be held in May, and the Summer Meeting at the Winfrith Atomic Energy establishment. The Society had acquired two silver cups from the English County Societies Conference, which had been discontinued the previous autumn.

Gordon reported that the Society's new tie and badge had been rapidly sold out, but he had difficulty reordering the button hole badge because he had been unable to discover who the manufacturer had been who had the original die. He had therefore, ordered some transfer badges for use on car windscreens. Gordon's letters were simply personal letters from him to the members. He was interested in the history of the Society, and its previous personalities. In his April 1981 letter he says that since taking over as Secretary he had been 'mystified' by the lack of historical documents belonging to the Society; 'prior to the 60's such things as Committee and AGM minutes do not exist.' He appealed to members to let him have any useful documents, and thanked Bob Laurenson for letting him have Year Books from 1935, asking if anyone had any copies of any earlier date. This provided the basis for the almost complete collection the Society now has. He read the back numbers of the Year Book and passed on anything he thought would interest the members. From the 1935 issue he found an article about the unveiling in April, 1934, of 'a two ton, 6 feet high, monolith block of grey granite, erected by the Society of Dorset Men...over the grave of Mr. Charles Rogers...fondly known as 'Wold Charles'.

The building of the atomic energy plant at Winfrith.

Gordon also reported on county events, especially when they were controversial. When the Central Electricity Generating Board issued a press statement in February 1980 saying that they were considering two sites in Dorset; Herbury near Weymouth and Winfrith Heath as locations for nuclear power stations without having consulted the Atomic Energy Authority at Winfrith, he expressed the view that 'they could not have chosen a site which will arouse more opposition. Undoubtedly members of the Society will wish our name to be associated with those opposing the use of this particular site, in spite of the attractions it may have for the CEGB.' The Society's Summer Meeting the following June was a visit to the Atomic Energy Establishment at Winfrith where they enjoyed a buffet lunch and a conducted tour.

The increasing activities of British Gas in extracting oil from Poole Harbour and the Wytch Farm site attracted his attention and concern at the effect this was having on the Dorset coast. In April, 1982, he told the members, 'Currently there are at least two major issues affecting the County, which are causing some local concern; one is an increase in the Parliamentary constituencies, whilst the other, the prospects of a new nuclear power station being sited in the County.' The Boundary Commission were proposing that Christchurch should be added as a new constituency and that North West Dorset should be extended from Shaftesbury to Lyme Regis, and that Dorchester and Weymouth should be joined together as one constituency. Everything that affected the County mattered to Gordon, and he considered it to be of interest to the Society; he even commented on the Falkland War, saying that, 'With the Naval Base at Portland, the Marines at Poole, and the Fleet Air Arm base at Yeovilton just over the border, Dorset was particularly affected.'

In September, 1982, he was delighted to tell the members that 'one of our members, Anthony Jolliffe...was a possible candidate for election to Lord Mayor 'of London, and that the Committee had decided to demonstrate the Society's support by taking part in the Lord Mayor's Show.

The Lord Mayor's Show
NOVEMBER 13th 1982

AFTER many months of preparation, on November 13th the Society were represented by a float in a very colourful Lord Mayor of London's Procession to honour our Life Member, Weymouth-born Alderman Sir Anthony Jolliffe, who was elected the 655th Lord Mayor of London. The float called 'Toast the Sons of Dorset', depicted a thatched pub with a bar where the Dorset folk group, 'The Yetties', (Bonnie Sartin, Pete Shutler and Mac McCullock) provided the Dorset music, whilst a group of Members and wives dressed as Edwardian country folk, did the toasting, with 'Ram Rod', a Dorset Horn Ram with Shepherd (Mr. John Randall) and smocked Yokels at rear. The theme of the Lord Mayor's procession was 'The Best of Britain' — what could be better than that Dorset should be represented?

The Society was supported by the resources of the Dorchester brewers Messrs. Eldridge Pope & Co., the float having been constructed in the brewery workshops to a design by Ronald Homes; the thatching was carried out by David Howell. Both come from the Shaftesbury area.

The entry was selected for interview by BBC television along the processional route, and was watched on a sunny day by vast crowds and televised to millions of people.

We offer our warmest thanks to Messrs. Eldridge Pope and to all members of the Society who gave financial support to this project.

To celebrate the occasion, Eldridge Pope have brewed a special beer called 'The Lord Mayor of London's Dorset Brew', and for every bottle sold, 2p will go to the Royal Society for Mentally Handicapped Children and Adults, the charity which Sir Anthony has adopted for his year in Office.

The programme entry read as follows :

Item 89 — The Society of Dorset Men.

Two of Dorset's traditions join to toast success to the new Lord Mayor, a Son of Dorset. The Society of Dorset Men, founded in 1904, includes Thomas Hardy among its Past Presidents.

Huntsman Ales have been brewed in Dorchester for even longer and are now quenching London thirsts. Hardy wrote of Dorchester's strong beer: 'It was of the most beautiful colour that the eye of an artist in beer could desire . . .'

D.470/5/1/1
The Lord Mayor's party at his dinner at the Mansion House for the Society of Dorset Men
Photographer: Western Gazette - May 1983

D.470/5/1/2
Diners at the dinner given by the Lord Mayor of London for the Society of Dorset Men
Photographer: Colin Hoare, Childe Okeford
May 1983

After the Lord Mayor's Show

The Jolliffe Years

AT the Annual General Meeting in May, 1984, Simon Wingfield Digby, who had been the President since 1970, retired, and Sir Anthony Jolliffe was elected in his place. He took the opportunity provided by the September Newsletter to write a personal letter to the members saying how honoured he felt by his election, and that his intentions for the Society were that it should grow, and that its members should take a more active part in its affairs, and 'to see that the County of Dorset is promoted for the benefit of all those who live in Dorset in general and for industry in Dorset in particular...I hope that the Society of Dorsetmen can become a forum where the people of Dorset can have a voice in the affairs of the nation and where applicable, have their thoughts represented in Government circles.'

Sir Anthony Jolliffe, the longest serving President of the Society, was born in Weymouth, where his great grandfather had been the coxswain to the Weymouth lifeboat and a local fisherman. After attending Porchester school in Bournemouth he qualified as a chartered accountant in London, where he started his own accountancy firm which rapidly expanded and now has offices in several cities in the United Kingdom as well as offices and businesses in over a dozen countries around the world, including factories in China. He was elected an Alderman for the City of London in 1973. He was appointed a Knight Grand Cross of the Order of the British Empire by Her Majesty the Queen in October, 1982. He was commissioned as a Deputy Lieutenant of Dorset in 2006, and officially welcomed the Queen on her visit to Weymouth in 2009.

In September, 1988, the Secretary was pleased to be able to say that 'I have at last, the majority of Members' Names and Addresses on Computor Disk' but so many alterations had needed to be made to the list that the system was not yet operational. Then, the following year, 1989, he announced that 'This year, all our social meetings are open for both ladies and guests.' The members' list, which the Membership Secretary was finding difficult in keeping up-to-date, because of members lapsing their membership or failing to notify of a change of address, was, in 1991, taken out of the Year Book and produced for the first time as a separate booklet.

Proposed changes for local government in Dorset by a special Commission, were debated at the Annual General Meeting in April, 1994. These were for new unitary councils; the Commission's preference being for three, consisting of Bournemouth and Christchurch, Poole, and the remainder of rural Dorset. The alternative suggestion was for four: Bournemouth and Christchurch, Poole, Eastern

Dorset and Western Dorset. All those present at the meeting except one voted for no change from the existing two-tier system. 'But', the Secretary said, 'It appears that the Commission has given more weight to the views of the county and district councils than to the representations received from the people of Dorset.'

The Society's centenary in July, 2004, was celebrated in great style at a lunch held in the Headquarters Officers' Mess of the Royal Signals Corps at Blandford Camp, where 315 members, wives and partners enjoyed a splenid meal. The President, Sir Anthony Jolliffe, told the gathering, 'Today we start on our next 100 years and go from strength to strength. Let us put the Great back into Great Britain. The Society believes in upholding all the standards and traditions of our fine country and we must hand on to all our traditions, in which we all believe.' He had earlier read a letter from Her Majesty the Queen in which she had sent 'all her best wishes to all those who are present at this notable occasion.' The toast of 'Dorset Our County' was proposed by Vice Admiral Sir Barry Wilson KGB, a member of the Society, who had retired from the Royal Navy as Flag Officer Sea Training at Portland. He then spoke on some aspects of the history of the Society and its famous personalities and the exploits of the various armed forces stationed in Dorset during these times. He recalled that the guest speaker at the 50th. Anniversary of the Society had been the broadcaster Ralph Wightman who had told members 'remember we have a wonderful county in Dorset – we have a history, a beauty and a culture.'

Having served the Society as its Secretary for 25 years - a quarter of its existence – Gordon Hine decided that the centenary year was time for him to retire. In his final Newsletter, he looked back to the beginnings of the Society as recorded in the first Year Books. He quoted from the address given at the first Annual General Meeting by the Chairman, J.C. Swinburn-Hanham JP, identifying himself with its sentiments; 'He looked forward to a long life for the Society. There would be Dorset Men as long as the world lasted, and there ought to be a Dorset Society as long as there were Dorset Men.' At the County Dinner in October, the President presented Gordon with a silver claret jug and thanked him for his 50 years of loyalty and service to the Society.

The Society elected Hayne Russell to be its new Secretary. Hayne was born in Dorchester, and attended Dorchester Grammar School. His father was a cabinet maker with the firm of Shepherd and Hedges, where he achieved fame as the maker of the casket in which the heart of Thomas Hardy was buried. On leaving school

The President and the Chairman cut the 2004 Centenary Cake

Hayne joined the Dorset Constabulary as a police cadet. After national service with the Coldstream Guards he rejoined the Dorset Police and served with the CID, becoming Chief Superintendent and retiring as Weymouth's divisional commander. He joined the Society in 1987 and in 2000 became its Membership Secretary.

The writing and producing of the Newsletter was taken on by Michel Hooper-Immins, a Weymouth man and a member of the Society since 1977. A professional journalist and an excellent photographer, with his skill the Newsletters immediately took on a new and professional appearance; no longer a two-paged typed sheet, they expanded to four pages and became a professionally printed publication using colour and photographs of events and personalities, providing an unbroken record of the Society up to the present day.

At the Centenary Year AGM. The Chairman, Roy Adam, reported that the Society was 'in a very healthy state in every way.' Membership had increased to over 1,200. He paid tribute to the retiring Secretary, Gordon Hine, for his twenty-five years service to the Society, saying that when Gordon had taken over in 1979, the Society was in poor straits and still based in London. In his address to members, Gordon said that he had joined the committee in 1958 and when he had become Secretary the Society 'hovered on the brink of bankruptcy' and 'The Society was now flourishing.'

Roy Adam had also played a significant part in the rebuilding of the Society and especially in the Annual Dinner. Roy became the MC for the event in 1983, and his lively charisma, his abilty to cheerfully lift the spirits and dispel any stuffiness out of what might otherwise be a too stiff and formal event, with his endless supply of funny stories told in his inimitable Dorset tones, transformed it into the major highlight of the year. Roy had also been the most regular recipient of the Society's Challis Cup awarded each year at the County Dinner to the member who had recruited the most new members during the year. His personality had become so central to the life of the Society that it was with shock and considerable dismay that its members heard that in January 2009 Roy had suffered a severe stroke. At the AGM in April, The President expressed the 'great sadness' of the members at the news and announced that 'Roy Adam will be unable to continue his vital role within the Society, but will always be warmly welcomed at any of our events.' Roy's son, Stuart, who had been assisting his father as Deputy Chairman and who took the chair at the meeting was therefore unanimously elected as the Society's Chairman. The meeting also agreed to set up a subcommittee to consider donations to Dorset charities. At the October Dinner the President presented a framed testimonal to Roy and a decanter containing Roy's favourite whisky and an inscribed whisky glass to Stuart to present to his father who was too unwell to attend. Roy was made an Honorary Deputy President for his services to the Society.

At the County Dinner the following year, 2010, the President, Sir Anthony Jolliffe, announced that after twenty-seven years he would retire from office at the AGM in April, 2011. He had served the Society as its President longer than any of his predecessors. In making his statement he said 'I stand down at a time when the Society has never been stronger and I am sure that under the guidance of a new President, together with your excellent Chairman, Stuart Adam, the Society will go from strength to strength in the years ahead.' At the AGM, the members unanimously elected as their next, and seventeenth President, Julian, now Lord Fellowes of West Stafford, who had been created a Life Peer in the New Year Honours List and officially taken his place in the House of Lords on 13 January 2011. He had first attended a Society function in its centenary year, as a guest speaker. He then became a member and was subsequently appointed a Deputy President. The retiring President, who had expressed his intention to continue to give the Society his support, saying 'The Society of Dorset Men will always have a place in my heart', was elected as a Deputy President, together with James Weld of Lulworth Castle. At the Annual Dinner in October, held in the newly built George Albert Hotel at Warden Hill, the new President presented Sir Anthony Jolliffe with a Testimonial of Thanks on behalf of the members for his 27 years of service to the Society, and a Mont Blanc fountain pen. The Chairman, Stuart Adam, paying tribute to Sir Anthony, said 'It is widely thought that the fortunes and profile of the Society changed for the better when Sir Anthony became Lord Mayor of London in 1982 and we thank him most sincerely for all he has achieved for us.'

In 2012 the Society marked the Diamond Jubilee of the Queen's accession to the throne with a garden party at Minterne House, at the invitation of Lord and Lady Digby. The Queen had suggested that organisations might like to plant a tree to mark her Jubilee, so, in an act of commemoration, the Society planted a Cedar of Lebanon in the grounds close the where the Queen herself had planted a tree on a visit to Minterne. Lord Digby had chosen the tree to replace several cedars which had been lost from the estate. Lord Digby welcomed the members of the Society in the Trafalgar Room of the House and told them something of the history of the

Digby family. He said: "I am really delighted to welcome the Society of Dorset Men to Minterne House. When my ancestors came here the surroundings were wild, but 200 years of hard work has created a wonderful garden.'

The formal act of planting was carried out by the former Chairman, Roy Adam and the current Chairman, his son Stuart. The Society's Chaplain then read words of dedication saying 'This tree is placed here today to mark the Diamond Jubilee of Elizabeth our Queen. May it grow strong and tall and stand for years to come as a tribute to Her Majesty and as a witness to this Society's wish to honour her for her 60 years of service and devotion to our nation and to the Commonwealth; for the way she has, through her gracious personality and example, contributed greatly to our national life and represented us as our Sovereign, winning respect and admiration throughout the world. May God bless her with good health and, as she continues to be the symbol which unites us as one nation, may she know the love, loyalty and devotion of all her people. Amen.

This was Roy Adams last public duty on behalf of the Society. In December, 2014, the members were shocked and saddened at the deaths within a few days of each other of both their longest serving Secretary, Gordon Hine, and Roy, their long time Chairman. Sir Anthony Jolliffe gave the tribute to each of them at their funeral thanksgiving services; for Gordon at Gillingham on 15 January and then for Roy at Blandford Parish Church on 23 January. Gordon had been a member of the Society for 61 years, having become a member in London in 1953. He became a member of the committee in 1958 and then Assistant General Secretary in 1972. Gordon served as a captain in the Royal Corps of Signals during the Second World War, first in India, then in Iraq and Syria, before joining the Campaign in the Western Desert. At the end of the War he was the signals officer in charge of the communications for the huge Victory Parade in London in 1946. After leaving the Army he completed his training as a Chartered Quantity Surveyor and in 1954 went to Australia for three years where he worked on the building preparations for the 1956 Olympic Games. Returning home to Dorset in 1962, he became a county, district and town councillor. He was three times Mayor of Shaftesbury and North Dorset district councillor for Motcombe and Ham from 1987 until 2007. He was a great supporter of good causes, raising thousands of pounds for charity through his Hine Collection of Mechanical Music; the dance, fairground and street organs he and his father had collected for over forty years. He was involved with the Shaftesbury Abbey and Museum Trust, a Director of Bournemouth Airport, John Foyle's Charity, Shaftesbury Carnival Committee, the Royal British Legion and the Shaftesbury Football Club. A member of the London Dorset Lodge for 54 years, he was made an honorary member in 2012.

Roy was born in Pimperne, near Blandford, and apart from his distinguished War service, he lived there the whole of his 91 years. When the War started he volunteered for the Royal Navy and joined Combined Operations. He was sent to train as a Commando in Scotland, and then served in Egypt, Malta and took part in the invasion of Italy at Taranto, and then, having joined J Force on the Isle of Wight, he took part in the D Day landings at Arromanches on 6 June 1944. When the War ended he returned home to Pimperne where he took an active part in village life as a pig farmer, pub landlord and local government officer. He was a member or clerk of the Pimperne Parish Council for 38 years and a Special Constable for 17 years. He was a member and supporter of many charitable and service organsations such as the Blandford Royal Navy Association and the RNLI. He took over from his father the organising of the annual Act of Remembrance at the memorial near Pimperne for the Collingwood Battalion of the Royal Naval Division which had served at Gallipoli, and continued to do this for 58 years. In 2000 he was awarded the MBE by the Queen for services to the community.

At a specially arranged lunch at the Crown Hotel in Blandford in May, 2015, Sir Anthony Jolliffe gave a large gathering of members an entertaining and fascinating account of his life and impressive career, from his family origins in Weymouth to his becoming Lord Mayor of London in 1982. A year or two after this high point in his life he suffered a drastic reversal of fortune, which necessitated him having to sell his cherished complete collection of Jaguar cars. From this dark period he succeeded in rebuilding his career, moving into engineering and seizing new opportunites to invest in business in China, with factories there and in other countries overseas. He is now head of a large Chinese management company with the Chinese Government as the sole client. He is in the process of writing his autobiography, which he hopes to have completed and published in 2016.

Dorset then and now

WHEN the Society began, in London in 1904, its aim was to reconnect Dorset Londoners with their home county. The Society is now based wholly in Dorset, and therefore it needs to be in touch with Dorset as it is today; a county which has inevitably seen many changes to its life and its landscape during the last 112 years.

In 1904, the Society's first President, Sir Frederick Treves, was enjoyng cycling to every part of the county for his book, The Highways and Byways in Dorset, published in 1906. In his Preface to the book, he imagines a visitor to the county standing on a hill overlooking the Blackmore Vale and looking 'down upon a country beyond of rare and romantic beauty. If they descend into these lowlands they will find that time has moved back a hundred years or so, and that they have stepped...into the England of the coaching days. In this Sleepy Hollow they will find the untroubled life of the past, will come

Cerne Abbas from "Highways and Byways"

upon such farmer's men as Gabriel Oak...Upon their ears too, will fall, like an echo from ancient England, the quaint speech of the dialect of Dorset.' The Dorset Treves sees and describes is still the rural Dorset of Hardy's Wessex; of Far From the Madding Crowd and The Woodlanders.

Whitechurch Canonicorum from "Highways and Byways"

This is still the Dorset of Arthur Mee's book about the county in The King's England series, published just before the Second World War in 1939. 'It is old, very old, and nature has richly endowed it...' 'One of the most distinctive of our English Shires, Dorset lies well apart.' 'Dorset is one of the least crowded of our counties, having about 623,000 acres with not quite a quarter of a million people on them. It is almost entirely a pastoral county, with dairies, sheep farming, poultry, gardens and fruit growing as its natural mainstays. There are also fisheries and quarries.'

The War brought a great influx of new people into the county. The German occupation of the Channel Islands brought many escaping islanders into Weymouth. The entry of the Americans into the War and the preparations for the D.Day

invasion of Europe in 1944 made Dorset, and especially the coastal towns of Studland, Swanage, Portland and Weymouth important strategic centres; crowded with troops and their equipment, and their harbours crammed with ships. Dorset was designated a major training and staging area, and the Dorset coast became a restricted zone. The Dorchester Barracks were assigned to the American troops and many soldiers were billeted in private homes. Between D Day, 6 June 1944, and the end of the European War on 8 May, 1945, 517,816 men and 144,093 vehicles crossed to Normandy from Weymouth and Portland. The impact of all this was considerable, and lasting. The black American troops were the first black men most of the Weymouth people had ever seen. They gave them a friendly welcome, as fellow human beings, which upset the white American soldiers who were strictly segregated from the black GIs. When these returned to America, they left behind some mixed race children, who with their families, are now part of the social mix of the local Dorset community.

The Shell Guide to Dorset by Michael Pitt-Rivers in 1966 referred back to the previous Shell Guide of 1935, written and illustrated by Paul Nash. Although it included much of what Nash had written, Pitt-Rivers wrote:

'The thirty years that have passed since he wrote The Face of Dorset have accounted for many alterations – and some blemishes – to that "Face". He deplored the thoughtless spread of housing by speculative builders. 'This has now been largely superseded by often ignorant and complacent local councils. The product is the same; building without design, without awareness of surroundings, without consideration for the aspect and the opportunities presented by the landscape.' Pitt-Rivers goes on to say 'The Dorset landscape has suffered a good deal since Paul Nash wrote in 1935...Acre for acre no county has suffered more from the spread of the Defence Establishments. Its dreadful buildings straddle the hills at Lulworth

Picture from Melbury Hill (courtesy of The National Trust)

and sprawl across the heathland further north...Dorset's future is in the balance. Poole is growing into a county borough...When Dorset loses Poole it may well lose its own viabilty as an administrative County. To counter this, and to ensure its own survival, the County Council is considering desperate measures: a new town in the Blackmore Vale nearly as big as Poole; expansion and industrialisation in many of Dorset's market towns; and instead of Poole's expansion (with Bournemouth) into a modern city, its containment within its existing boundaries. Such a plan may save the County Council but it would mean the end of rural Dorset.'

Very fortunately, these extreme planning attempts to solve the problem and balance the books were avoided. In 1974 central Government decided that Bournemouth and Christchurch should become part of Dorset, and then, in 1997, both Bournemouth and Poole, while remaining part of Dorset, became unitary authorities with separate Borough Councils in their own right. Of course, wrapping the Dorset boundary around Bournemouth and Christchurch did not immediately persuade the 183,000 new residents of Dorset that this was where they now truly belonged. Jo Draper, in her outstanding guide to the county, Dorset the Complete Guide published in 1986, says that 'the area had one third of the population of Dorset. (The other two thirds of the population would probably deny that these two towns are part of Dorset).' And with this the reluctant former residents of Hampshire would probably also agree. Although so closely forming one large conurbation with the ancient Dorset port of Poole, it is still the case that to their residents and most of the rest of Dorset, Bournemouth and Christchurch may be in Dorset, but they are, not yet, of it.

The author, John Fowles, a resident of Lyme Regis, provided a Foreword for Dorset, the Complete Guide. In this Fowles writes, 'Dorset can...count itself happy. It remains the gentlest, the most classically balanced of the four South Western counties...The county is not least lucky in the fact that by far its largest conurbation, made up of Poole, Bournemouth and Christchurch, lies on its eastern fringe. No unwieldy city, or even, by national standards, over-large town, disturbs the rest of it. The county town, Dorchester, remains mercifully and beautifully small. It is still almost an eighteenth or nineteenth century provincial 'capital', ten thousand miles from London; and still a fitting home for its two most celebrated literary ghosts, those of William Barnes and Thomas Hardy.' But, stand on Maiden Castle today, and look back at Dorchester. The ancient heart of the town is almost obscured by the growth of buildings on either side; most unmissable, the Duchy of Cornwall's still expanding 'urban village' of Poundbury, where the old wheat fields of Middle Farm and Poundbury Farm, (described lovingly by Hardy in The Mayor of Casterbridge) were still, just twenty years ago. Brewery Square is also growing fast, incorporating some of the old Eldridge Pope buildings and surrounding them with blocks of apartments, shops, restaurants, hotels and a cinema on the old Brewery site next to the station, which it is planned to rebuild as the first solar powered station in the country.

Brewery Square, Dorchester

Dorset is now attracting far more visitors as a tourist destination than ever before. Twenty years ago, there was a regular T.V programme in which the husband and wife team who presented it, explored the most rural areas of the southern counties. Whenever they came to Dorset they would refer to it as 'the forgotten county.' Although those seeking family holidays on sandy beaches crowded into Dorset's popular seaside towns, many others would pass the tip of the county on their way down to Devon and Cornwall. This has now changed. The successful designation of the Dorset coastline in 2001 as the Jurassic Coast UNESCO World Heritage Site, with its uniquely important geological structure and history, and its

abundance of fossils of ancient sea creatures, has brought thousands more visitors to the county, which is now proudly proclaiming itself as 'The Home of the Jurassic Coast.' The Olympic Games in 2004 projected television views of Weymouth and Dorset daily to all the world. Popular television programmes and films such as 'Broadchurch' and 'Far From the Madding Crowd' made in the county, have boosted the tourist industry. Portland Harbour, no longer an important major naval base - though still servicing naval ships – is today attracting regular and increasing visits from ever larger cruise ships. On these the Americans are returning to Weymouth, to peacefully enjoy the delights of the town and to take tours to the surrounding countryside.

The population of the county is growing and increasingly diverse. In the twenty years from 1996 to 2016, the number of people living in the Dorset County Council area has grown from 379,500 to 418,300. The total population including Bournemouth and Christchurch increased from 676,000 to 759,800. According to National Statistics (2014) the projected growth over the next twenty-five years is 15.9%. The DCC Area, distinct from the Bournemouth Poole Christchurch conurbation, has a lower birth rate than England and Wales but a higher death rate. A higher average population of over 65s means there is growing pressure on adult and care services, and this is expected to increase as the number of people over 65 grows by 50% in the next twenty five years. The number of people born elsewhere than in the county is also increasing. The 2011 census for Dorset, including the conurbation, gives 88.2% born in the county with 11.8% not Dorset born. Of these, 1.7% came from the countries that were members of the European Union in 2001, and 1.6% from countries which were given accession to the EU in 2011. With the increasing number of Chinese, Indian, Thai and other exotic restaurants well established throughout the county, and people of many different races serving in shops and staffing our hospitals, and visitors coming from many parts of the world, (including recently, at least one from Tibet in Dorchester) the county now has a small but definite multicultural mix. The latest statistics on ethnicity in Dorset, (9 June 2016) give the Black and Minority Ethnic Population in Dorset as increasing from 3.2 % in 2001 to 4.4 % in 2011.The Dorset Multicultural Network is actively working with the different ethnic communities, and the Dorset Red Cross is busy meeting refugees and asylum seekers as they arrive at Bournemouth Airport - where 580 illigal immigrants have been detained - and helping immigrants being held in the Verne on Portland.

Yet, in spite of all the considerable changes to the appearance and social make up of the county, the Dorset landscape is still one of exceptional beauty and importance. 55.0% of the Dorset land area is designated as Areas of Oustanding Natural Beauty. The county has 135 Sites of Special Scientific Interest, nine Nature Reserves, and 91 kilometres of Heritage coastline. Within the county can be found 85.0 % of all the different species of mammals living in Britain, 90.0 % of all birds, 80.0% of all butterflies – only two other counties have as many – and nearly all the country's reptiles and amphibians. While being only 2.0% of the area of England Dorset has 5.0 % of the nationally protected monuments, 9,931 listed buildings,

239 conservation areas, 1,043 scheduled ancient monuments and 37 Historic Parks and Gardens. Although agriculture has declined and is no longer the main industry in the county, Dorset is still mainly rural, with the the amount of land classified as agricultural actually increasing , due to more permanent grassland and to land which has been set aside. A visitor today, could still stand on the chalk downs, and look across the Blackmore and Marshwood Vales, at the ancient landscape of Dorset, and see a countryside that continues to be recognisable as the one Treves decribed in 1906, and is still, in essence, the heart of Thomas Hardy's Wessex, and William Barnes's 'Dorset Dear.'

The Society today

TODAY, this Society brings together 1,200 members who have a personal love for Dorset and a commitment to support all that is important for the best interests and well-being of the county and those who live in it. Individually, many of them are making their own active contribution to the life of the county, through their various professional lives and their involvement in their local communities and in wider ways. As members of this Society they are able to recognise a common bond and get to know and enjoy fellowship with others who share their devotion to Dorset. There are throughout the county, many separate organisations dedicated to particular needs and interests, and our members are among those who support these and bring to our Society their experience and knowledge, so that, through the informal contacts and friendships the Society enables its members to make, we learn more about the county from each other, and broaden our perspective on those things that are good and contribute to the quality of the county's life and well-being, as well as seeing and guarding against those things that are detrimental to it.

The Society's 112th Annual General Meeting was held in the north of the county at the Coppleridge Inn, Motcombe, near Shaftesbury. In April, 2016. The Chairman, Stuart Adam, extended a warm welcome to the members and their wives and partners. In his Chairman's Report, he said that at the start of the year we were placed in a difficult situation with having to find someone to take over the Editorship of the Year Book. Fortunately one of the members, Selwyn Williams, had come forward and produced an excellent 2016 Year Book. He reported on the events of the year which had included the 'fascinating and entertaining lunch' and the talk given by Sir Anthony Jolliffe, and the increasingly popular Christmas Lunch followed by carols, ably led by our Membership Secretary, Peter Lush. The Society's new Dorset Award, in the shape of the County, was on display for the members to see. Stuart also mentioned that this Illustrated History of the Society was in the process of being produced, and that we hoped it would be available for sale by September this year. He told the meeting 'with regret' that the Purbeck section of the Society had now ceased to meet because it had been unable to find new officers to replace the former Chairman and Secretary who had retired'. He paid tribute especially to the Purbeck's Secretary, Geoff King, thanking him for his long years of service to the Society, and announced that he would be made an honorary member. The Society's Honorary Secretary, Hayne Russell, now wished to retire, having held the office for twelve years, (since the centenary year in 2004) and this would therefore be his last year. An appeal was made for the members to suggest someone willing to take over from Hayne, who would be able to work alongside him 'to find out just what makes the Society tick!' The Chairman extended his grateful thanks and appreciation to all the officers and members of the Committee 'without whose help the Society could not function.' He extended a warm welcome to Dr. Paul Atterbury who had kindly accepted our offer to become a Deputy President of the Society.

The President and Chairman with the Society's Lectern

In his address, the Chairman reported that the Society's Charity Committee had 'continued to ensure that worthy Dorset charities receive our support,' and that during the year we had donated a total of £1,150. From the very early days the Society has supported the notion that where possible, help should by given to those members who might find themselves in difficulties. Therefore, amongst the four objects laid down at the Society's formation was one which stated that the Society would 'assist, by every means in its power, natives of Dorset who may stand in need of the influence and help of the Society.' This was put to good use when young men from Dorset arrived in London looking for work and found themselves in financial difficulties, not having been able to find employment there. The Society then had a large number of members living in London with Dorset roots and they were able to provide very welcome assistance to enable these aspiring young men to settle and find employment. During both world wars the Society provided comforts in the form of tobacco and warm clothing to members of the Dorset Regiment serving in the front line and to prisoners of war. Letters of appreciation received show that this was a most welcome gesture by the Society.

In order to advance this charitable objective to suit the modern day it was proposed in 2009 that the Society should form a small charity sub-committee with a view to giving some tangible help to Dorset organisations who might be in need of some financial help. After the matter had been discussed by the committee, a number of principles were agreed as follows:

1. The charity should be for the benefit to Dorset

2. Be of direct benefit to the people of Dorset

3. Be non-political

4. Support people, culture, sport and education

5. Priority given to youth based charities

6. Set up an initial fund of £5,000

7. Add a sum each year as agreed by the Committee

8. Additional funds raised at special Society events

9. Committee to decide either one main charity a year or a number of smaller ones

10. Invite speaker from the charity to attend a society function

11. Committee to decide on charity options

The sub-committee comprises the Hon. Treasurer and three committee members. One of the first donations made in 2009 was £500 to the Friends of Guiding on Brownsea Island to assist in the purchase of an electric buggy to help disabled visitors gain access to this wonderful jewel in Poole Harbour. Since then, a total of £7,700 has been handed to some 25 Dorset based organisations and the Society has benefited from some very welcome publicity. The Society Vice-Chairman, Andy Prowse, has had the happy task of travelling round the county giving out the cheques and seeing the grateful smiles on the faces of the recipients. In future, the Society will continue to strive and support many other worthy Dorset charities.

Photo of Brownsea Buggy

Among its social activities for the members, the Society encourages competition for a number of cups and awards. One of these, the Hambro Cup, was presented in 1938 by Captain Angus Hambro, DL. JP., who was President of the Society from 1925 until 1933, and then again from 1936 to 1944. He was also the M.P. for North and South Dorset at different times and a very fine golfer. He was Captain of the Royal and Ancient, an International and South West Amateur Champion and semi-finalist in the Amateur Championship. This very fine silver cup was presented to be played for annually, and the first winner, in 1939, was R. Warren. Competition for this was interrupted by the war, which meant that it was not played for again until1962. Then for a number of years the competition was played at the Royal Mid-Surrey Golf Club, and members were encouraged to come from Dorset and elsewhere, and, after a day's golf, to attend the London Dinner where the cup was presented. The competition is now played at the Came Down Golf Course and is proving to be a very popular event among the golfing members of the Society.

In 1952, an overseas member, Mr. Brian Challis, who had lived in Kenya for a number of years, visited this country and attended the London Dinner. He announced at the Dinner that he would be presenting a silver cup to the Society and suggested that it be awarded each year to the member who recruited the most new members. Since that year the cup has been awarded according to the wishes of the late Brian Challis at the County Dinner and bears a list of all the winners. Since 1908, new members have been able to obtain the Society's badge, with its Society motto 'Who's A'fear'd?', and this has only been slightly modified today. The London members also designed a Society tie. The present tie now has a striped design and there is also a blazer badge and cuff links for members to obtain and wear at Society functions.

The Society's special new award is for any resident of Dorset who has achieved something exceptional for the benefit of the county. This will be an occasional award, to be presented only when someone, either male or female, can be recognised as having made an outstanding contribution to the county, which has enhanced and promoted its wider reputation. It has been decided that the first recipient of this award is to be the distinguished geomorphologist, Professor Denys Brunsden,

OBE, DSc., FKC (Emeritus Professor, King's College, London) who proposed the Dorset and East Devon Coast for World Heritage Site status at a Lyme Bay Forum meeting in 1994. This was granted in 2001. He has been invited to be the Society's guest at the Annual Dinner in October, 2016, when he will be presented with the award by the Society's President, Lord Fellowes.

Invited to look forward to the future of the Society as we come to the end of this book, Stuart Adam wrote:

The Society of Dorset Men remains very strong despite having to face up to a number of challenges experienced by most similar organisations. Although new members continue to came forward and join we are conscious of the fact that we have an ageing membership and young people have many competing interests. This may mean making changes but we must ensure that the aims and traditions which have served so well since the Society's beginnings in 1904 are not surrendered. We have a small band of members who work hard to service our membership and new technology has vastly improved our ability to keep members informed and ensure our records etc., are accurate. Our functions remain well supported so we look forward to a long and bright future for our Society.

The President, members and guests at the Annual General Meeting and Lunch
at the Coppleridge Inn, Motcombe, 10th April 2016
Photo by Terry Fisher

The President, Lord Fellowes,
Christine & Anthony Oliver MBE

The President, Lord Fellowes
welcoming Dr. Paul Atterbury
as the new Deputy President
at the Society's lectern and the
Society's new special award.

Chrissie & Dr. Paul Atterbury, Paul Hooley MBE JP

Jeannie Steven, Sam Woodcock, A. Stephens-Holly

John Rousell, Douglas & Lynda Beazer

Val & Ian Morton, Geoff King

Ellie & David Lloyd, Alderman Andy Hutchings

Stuart & Sharon Cullingford, Robin & Esther Hussey

Photos taken at the Society's A.G.M. in April 2016

by Michel Hooper-Immins

ENVOI

As we reach the end of this book – though by no means the end of this story – as Chaplain as well as Historian to this Society, I feel that the most appropriate way for me to close this history, is with the prayer that we use each year when we meet at the graves of our Founder Secretary and our Founder President to honour their memories and to pay tribute to them. The prayer is not just for them and for those who have followed them in this Society, but also for all who love our County and who wish it well.

Almighty God, we remember before you, all those who out of love for our County, founded our Society, and through their lives, served this Society, our County and our Nation with distinction and honour. As we thank you for their lives and example, we pray that we and all who belong to this Society, and all who hold our County dear, may continue to honour their memories by maintaining the traditions of service and love for Dorset which they established and passed on to us; that this small but beautiful part of our Nation may continue to be a place where the best qualities of our national life may be upheld and valued. Amen.